CONTENTS

INTRODUCTION

On opening this book, some people may think 'oh, yet another cookery book'. Yes and no, might be the reply. This ambiguous and very "Norman" response is not motivated by a desire to pay tribute to a province which has contributed a great deal to French gastronomy ("la marmite dieppoise", "le poulet Vallée d'Auge", "le ris de veau normande", Livarot and Camembert cheese etc., not to mention cider and calvados) but is merely stating the truth.

To go further, we do, in fact, want to emphasize all the things that this book does and does not want to be. The reader will not find here any sophisticated recipes ("mousse de sardines aux fruits de la passion" - sardine mousse with passion fruit!), or anything that is too complicated ("macaronis farcis à la purée de truffes" - macaroni stuffed with truffle purée !) to be tackled by the individual without a feeling of dread. There are lots of other books which aim to enable the aspiring amateur to rise (or almost) to the level of the renowned master chefs (a lot of media coverage is devoted to these books). On the contrary, the language used, and the techniques described here, all aim to be at the level of the amateur cook who just wants to give his family and friends a little pleasure by cooking some recipes which, although they are often traditional, are gradually disappearing from sight.

We have tried to keep it simple and practical and to this end we have given, whenever possible, certain "tricks of the trade" which are liable to make the job easier. We have systematically used the simplest of terms, working on the principle that a technique is much easier to practice if its internal mechanism has been properly understood. We have endeavoured to show why such and such operation must be carried out in such and such a way. Simplicity, common sense and understanding are key words for absorbing the concept that cooking is an art (or a science - this can be discussed ad infinitum!) where organisation plays a vital and decisive role, granted, of course, that nature should not be forced and that each individual must go at his own pace.

With this in mind, we have tried to keep the use of professional technical terms to a minimum and where we have been forced to use them we have also given a simple definition. Likewise, the reader will notice that the cooking times given are flexible, since the modern cook now has a choice of cooking apparatus which vary greatly according to the type of energy used - gas, electricity, microwaves, induction hobs. Since the latter are still a rarity, due to their price, and are thus little known by the individual cook, we have hardly mentioned them. On the other hand, we must recognize the fact that the microwave is a marvellous tool for reheating dishes which have been prepared in advance (apart from food which has been grilled!) but that "simmering" is still the prerogative of gas cooking as the intensity of the heat can be precisely regulated by eye, such as is not the case with electricity.

Equally, with regard to which products to use, this book wishes to take into consideration the incredible transformations which have taken place on the technical front over the last ten years or so. Freezing techniques have enabled the cook to use products which, in many cases, can be used as if they were fresh, provided that guidelines for defrosting are properly respected. Alternatively, for some other products, it is very risky to use anything but fresh produce as defrosting affects the structure of the fibres i.e. of vegetables.

On previous pages:
Savoy, the land of cheese, is also the land of the delicatessen, to suit a myriad of tastes.

Before tackling the heart of the subject, that is to say the recipes, we would like to say something about the way in which the book is laid out.

Firstly we have made some observations which we think are useful with regard to the complex question of seasoning (spices, herbs, sauces). We strongly recommend that the reader pays a great deal of attention to this part of the book for this subject constitutes a vital part of getting to know (and love!) french cooking.

Next, in the traditional manner, the reader will find recipes for soups, hot and cold entrées, fish, meat, vegetables, some suggestions for cheeses and desserts, and finally, recipes for dishes which have become veritable myths of French cookery and which can each, individually, serve as a proper meal.

All the titles used correspond closely to the contents: egg mayonnaise is not referred to as "the pleasure of Christopher Columbus clothed in golden cream" nor is "coq au vin" referred to as "the king of the farmyard à la Bacchus" nor is vegetable soup described as a "thick creamy sauce made with the delights of the forest".

And now, good luck with the cooking and bon appetit for the eating! Our sole ambition is that the reader should get as much pleasure from using this book as we have had in writing it.

APROPOS
OF SEASONING:
herbs, spices, marinades, sauces

The reader will notice that the recipes contained in this book do not give instructions as to the amount of salt to be used and this requires an explanation. The author has deliberately not used salt for more than thirty years now, and replaces this ingredient with various others, about which we will now go on to say a few words.

Allow us to use a quotation (this will be the only one in this work); it is from Marc Meneau in "La Cuisine en fêtes" (1986 p. 24) and if we refer to it, it is both because it reflects an excellent statement of the principle and because it has served as an encouragement to the author of these lines who did, in fact, prepare this recipe of warm courgettes for his friend Meneau:
"How sad to see a guest cover the dish, that you have so lovingly prepared, with salt and pepper. Some do this without even having tasted the food! In times past in France, food was hardly salted, all that was used was the flavouring of each individual food, one highlighted by another. One of my friends, a passionate cook, prepares his dishes without any salt, simply by gathering flavours together. Once, he had me taste a salad of warm courgettes seasoned with poppy seeds, the result was admirable!"

Let us work then on a double principle - salt your plate to your own taste and try to find ways of replacing salt during cooking with other ingredients which "add flavour", taking into consideration the fact that foods already include salt in their natural state..

HERBS AND SPICES

Which ingredients can serve as a replacement for salt? There are so many that we must be content with a limited list of some of the herbs and spices available along with some observations about them.

First of all **pepper.** Let us immediately banish one of the myths which surrounds this subject - the colour does not correspond to a particular type of pepper but to a stage in its maturity and processing. The grains (twenty or so per head on this climbing plant) are green before they are fully ripened and it is only due to fashion that they are harvested then, so that they can be sold deep frozen or in pickled preparations. Normally these grains turn black (grey pepper is harvested a little before it is ripe) and white pepper is only white because the outer pulp has been removed. White pepper is popular because it does not colour sauces like black pepper does. Coarsely ground pepper is called "mignonette" and is used, in particular, in the preparation of "steak au poivre" (see page...) and for pepper sauce.

Not to be confused with pepper is the product which is improperly called "cayenne pepper". This is, in fact, the powder of a very powerful red pepper.

Of the spices, let us pick out **saffron,** with regard to which, it is also necessary to dissipate an illusion. The product which is generally known by this name in France is not really saffron but is more like turmeric in its aromatic odour and its peppery taste. This confusion can easily be explained by the fact that it takes 100 000 crocus flowers to get 1 000 grams of dried powder (and 1 kilogram costs approx. £ 1,200).

Real **curry** (carry, karry etc.) also has little to do with the product that is sold in Europe. It is the result of a subtle mixture of various spices (cardamom, turmeric, ginger and coriander at least, and often other spices as well, but the exact composition still remains a secret!).

Ginger must be used with care, not because of its powers as an aphrodisiac, but because it has a pronounced taste and makes the flavour of other ingredients disappear. The same goes for **nutmeg** and **cinnamon.** It is all a question of proportioning the ingredients and it is up to you to experiment with them yourself!

Contrary to what many people think **quatre-epices (allspice)** is not the result of a mixture of spices, it is, in fact, the powdered fruit of an herbaceous plant which can grow as tall as a tree.

Let us say a little, in passing, about **mustard.** This is obtained by grinding the seeds of a one metre high herbaceous plant, which are then soaked in red or white wine, or vinegar or a mixture of the two. The differences between brands comes from the choice of liquid used and the proportions of the mixture. For several decades now, a great number of flavoured mustards have been developed (with tarragon, with herbs, with red fruits, green pepper, etc.) which allow for multiple combinations in the preparation of some sauces.

What is there to say about **"fines herbes" (herbs for seasoning)**? Too often they are underestimated yet their use means that salt can be used less and gives the dish a certain individuality thereby adding value for the cook. Certain precautions must, however, be taken. Do not misuse these herbs, watch out for the harmonies of taste which exist between them, do not use the chopping board and definitely not the mixer. Why? Because only cutting them up with scissors stops the juice from escaping when the leaves are cut. Try it, you will notice the difference!

Tarragon, basil, rosemary, sage, thyme - these are the products which you should have at hand when preparing some of the dishes. Use these herbs fresh or frozen rather than in their powdered form. One easy and effective formula is the use of bouquet garni (bay leaves, thyme and parsley combined together) which is very handy when preparing stock (i.e. for pot-au-feu, but not just for this).

MARINADES

The marinade, that is to say, initially a mixture of water and vinegar, with salt (the name comes from the "sel marin" or sea salt which was used) and pepper, was originally used only for soaking the meat of large game, prior to cooking. Little by little, various spices and aromatics were added to the mixture and it was used not only for game but also for some culinary preparations (meat for terrines or for ragouts, with some fish). Nowadays, the fact that game can be frozen, has meant that marinades are used more than ever, since all game (except pigeon) is defrosted in a sweet marinade for 48 h at 4-7°.

The composition of a basic marinade (basic because it is always possible to add any spice or herb to it) is as follows:

• For 1 litre of red or white wine: 1/2 glass of wine vinegar, 3 tablespoons of oil, 2 thinly sliced onions, 2 cloves of garlic, 2 cloves, 5 peppercorns, 1 bay leaf, 1 small stick of celery, 1 sprig of thyme, 2 thinly sliced carrots.

It should be noted that marinades made with white wine do not mask the flavour of the meat as much as those made with red wine.

This marinade is recommended equally as well for use with fresh game.

It is possible to cook this marinade prior to use (bring to the boil and then simmer for 30 minutes). If you do, make sure that it has cooled down properly before using it as a sauce.

It is never advisable to use metal pans (except stainless steel) for a marinade because they can produce an unpleasant taste that can taint the meat. It is preferable to use stoneware, earthenware or enamel. Likewise, use wooden utensils for stirring the contents of the marinade.

SAUCES

We hear a lot about "nouvelle cuisine" but this wave of fashion is already beginning to ebb. Things are not, however, swinging too far in the opposite direction of excess. In our opinion, the essential innovation of this "nouvelle cuisine" does not lie in the excessively sophisticated nature of the recipes or in the outlandish affectation in the colour and presentation of the dishes (i.e. the often ridiculous use of a dish cover when the portion being protected by it is pitifully meagre for anyone with a normal appetite), but in the overall rejection of the use of flour in sauces and a reduction in the use of fats, all of which goes against the grain of time honoured tradition.

What is a sauce? It is an intimate mixture of several ingredients, a rather liquid combination of foods. Roughly speaking, there are three separate ingredients: the proteins (the base) which give the sauce its foundation (oil for mayonnaise, milk for béchamel, butter for hollondaise etc.), the spices which are added in varying numbers and, finally, the binding which exists in order to thicken the watery solution.

Most sauces can be divided into two categories: those which are not thickened (a typical example being the vinaigrette) and those which are thickened. "Historically" speaking, the most frequently used thickening ingredient has been starch in the form of flour or potato starch. Egg yolk is also a thickening agent.

If flour has had (and still does have) a great deal of success as a thickening agent, it is due to its stabilising qualities. There is, in fact, a temperature limit for sauces which are thickened when hot, above which there is a possibility that the ingredients of the sauce will separate (the sauce "turns") if flour has not been used, as this prevents such destabilization.

The greatest innovation of modern cooking (and this innovation goes back to the years preceding the last World War, thanks to chefs such as André Guillot, and not to the blustering and media oriented articles appearing in certain magazines in the sixties) has been the elimination of flour and the movement toward a lighter form of cooking where sauces are thickened by reduction, which is sometimes accentuated by the use of cream. In addition, we must consider the fact that individual cooks can now use stocks, for sauces to accompany meats and vegetables, which used to be reserved only for the professionals and about which we must say a few words (these can be found on sale under the name of meat extracts and in the form of pastes or liquids).

Stocks for sauces are called by different names according to their degree of concentration. They constitute both the basis of the sauce and also the thickening ingredient. The first step in the preparation of the stock is the meat juice, obtained by adding hot water or white wine to the residue left after cooking the meat, then the actual veal stock itself, then the "demi-glace" and finally the "glace". In order to obtain a real "fond de veau" (veal stock) you will need 1 or 2 kg of calf's bones, some carrots, some leeks, some herbs (thyme, bay, parsley, celery leaves, garlic cloves etc.) all of which should be covered with water and then simmered for about 8 hours. The stock is said to be white if it is made as above and "tout court" or brown if all the ingredients, especially the bones, have been browned on a tray in the oven beforehand. The demi-glace is obtained by reducing the liquid for a further 5 hours and the glace by reducing for another hour. In order to gain some idea of the importance of the reduction you should be aware that from 10 litres (stock), you get 2 litres (demi-glace) and 1 litre (glace).

Sauce aïoli

If you use the meat extracts that we talked about earlier you must be aware that these correspond to the actual stock itself and not to the glace or the demi-glace. The amateur cannot hope to get demi-glace or glace from this extract as reducing it would end up in an excessively salty solution.

The thing which gives the sauces prepared by great chefs the edge, is the quality of their stocks, the slow preparation and the composition of which remain closely guarded secrets.

A word about the "coulis". This word has, in culinary terms, quite a vague meaning. In ancient works (up until the beginning of the XX th century) it was used to describe sauces in general. Nowadays, a "coulis" corresponds more to certain sauces which are prepared as follows:

• For "coulis de lentilles" (lentil purée) : sweat pieces of carrot and ham until they are caramelized; add the cooked lentils, put through a conical strainer and add to the stock;
• For "coulis de navets" (turnip purée) : cook the turnips until they are golden brown; add some bouillon in order to obtain a thick, lumpy purée; put through a conical strainer.

SOME RECIPES FOR SAUCES

GARLIC PUREE

• Place 15 peeled and crushed cloves of garlic (remove the film which appears after crushing) in a small saucepan; add 1 tablespoon of water and 1 tablespoon of crème fraîche; cover and cook on a low light for 15 to 20 minutes. Put the whole lot through a conical strainer.

ANOTHER GARLIC SAUCE

• Cook 20 cloves of unpeeled garlic in aluminum foil in the oven (30 mins, 200m or gas mark 6). Soak 50 g of stale breadcrumbs in 25 cl of bouillon; peel the cooked garlic and 2 large cloves of raw garlic. Crush the lot and pound into the breadcrumbs; add ginger (1/2 teaspoonful), cinnamon (same quantity). Allow to boil for several minutes and then put through a conical strainer.

CREAM OF SHALLOTS

• Finely chop about 50 g of shallots; cut up 6 to 8 leaves of fresh tarragon with scissors and place these two ingredients in a small saucepan with a little dry white wine. Reduce until the mixture has the appearance of a purée. Add 25 cl of crème fraîche and leave to cook on a low light for 10 minutes. Then beat in 125 g of butter in small pieces. Put the whole mixture through a conical strainer.

Sauce hollandaise

HOLLANDAISE SAUCE

• For a long time this sauce was the dread of all cooks as the butter has a tendency to "turn to oil" according to its composition and whether or not a (variable) temperature threshold is exceeded. Nowadays, we have special pieces of equipment - "sauciers", which enable us to make hollandaise sauce very easily, provided that we follow instructions closely. Here, however, for traditionalists (and for the courageous) is the traditional recipe for hollandaise sauce.

• Place 3 tablespoons of wine vinegar, 1 tablespoon of water, 3 finely chopped shallots and a pinch of pepper in a saucepan (not aluminium since eggs are to be used); heat and reduce until there is just a teaspoonful left. Allow to cool.

• Separate 3 egg yolks and beat with 2 tablespoons of water with a whisk in order to obtain an even mixture which can be poured into the saucepan. Place this in a very hot bain-marie and continue to beat all the surfaces of the saucepan with the whisk. This is where the difficulty lies, since you need to obtain a slightly runny mixture without using too high a temperature which will melt the butter into oil and solidify the egg yolks.

. There is, however, a method by which you can avoid all the anguish involved in awaiting the success of the operation - when you have finished reducing the

vinegar and shallots etc., add 100 g of crème fraîche, bring to the boil and reduce by one third. Next add 200 g of butter cut into pieces and place over a high heat. The butter will be stabilised thanks to the moistness of the crème fraîche. The sauce will keep and can even be reheated as long as it is beaten with a whisk.

MAYONNAISE SAUCE

• This sauce is such an every day thing and is so well known that we hardly like to describe it.

• Before you do anything else, make sure that the various ingredients (egg yolks, oil, vinegar) are all at the same ambient temperature (do not take the eggs out of the fridge just before use!).

• Beat 2 egg yolks in a bowl with a wooden spoon (no metal utensils); pour in the oil (preferably olive oil but any oil will do), little by little, still turning the spoon. When the sauce has taken, add a thin stream of vinegar, salt and pepper and mix well (the vinegar, salt and pepper can be replaced by mustard).

MUSTARD SAUCE

• Mix together 1 tablespoon of glace or demi-glace (see page 12), 150 g of crème fraîche, 3 tablespoons of mustard and the juice of half a lemon. Heat whilst continuing to blend.

SAUCE BECHAMEL BASIC WHITE SAUCE

• Two recipes are given in order to show how the technique has evolved.

• In the "traditional" recipe: melt 40 g of butter; when this is hot add 40 g of flour. Mix together whilst adding, little by little, 2 large glasses of cold milk and continue to heat. Bring to the boil and add more milk if the sauce becomes too thick; after lowering the heat add 40 g of butter, leave on a low light and continue to mix together.

• In the "modern" recipe: heat 4 tablespoons of water with "la mignonette" (coarse-ground pepper); reduce by one half; add 30 cl of double cream, some pepper and some nutmeg. Reduce quickly on the highest heat available until the sauce thickens (6 to 7 minutes).

•**Caution:** use a large pan because when the mixture boils it may overflow. Take note of a "trick" which links the modern recipe with the traditional one. This is a means of stopping the sauce from "turning" when the temperature is lowered prior to serving. In order to stabilise the sauce you can use cornflour (this has the same effect as flour): 1 teaspoon dissolved in as much cold water, poured into the saucepan just before the mixture thickens.

BÉARNAISE SAUCE

• Bring 1 shallot, 2 tarragon leaves cut up very finely with scissors, several ground black peppercorns and 5 cl of vinegar, to the boil in a saucepan. Reduce; take the saucepan off the heat and add 1 tablespoon of cold water and allow to cool properly. Add 2 egg yolks and whisk.

• Put the saucepan back on the heat, but in a bain-marie. Continue to whisk the eggs and when they become frothy, mix in 180 g of butter in very small pieces (knobs). Put the sauce through a conical strainer as soon as it is frothy and has thickened.

• If you add 1 tablespoon of tomato purée to béarnaise sauce you get Choron sauce.

Sauce béarnaise

Pepper sauce

• Preparation of this sauce, which is used to accompany roast game (legs of venison), is delicate, and slow.

• It is, therefore, advisable to use a ready made pepper sauce (frozen). This does not stop you from improving it by adding it to the residue from the tray on which the game has been cooked and adding 2 or 3 tablespoons of cream.

• Also, there is a simplified version of the preparation. Brown the solid ingredients of the marinade used for the game, in oil, add the scraps or trimmings of the meat which were removed prior to marinading, add several tablespoons of meat stock, 2 ladlefuls of marinade and cook for 1 hour. Add pepper, paprika and several tablespoons of cream. Put the whole lot through a conical strainer and pour into the cooking dish to mix with the residue from the meat.

Sauce vinaigrette french dressing

• Mix together mustard (1 tablespoon), olive oil (3 tablespoons), vinegar or lemon juice (1 tablespoon), pepper and parsley which has been finely cut with scissors.

Aioli sauce

• Pound 4 peeled cloves of garlic in a mortar; mix in 1 egg yolk and continue, as if for mayonnaise, with the olive oil. As the consistency of the aioli is more fluid than mayonnaise, 1 teaspoon of cold water and/or the juice of a lemon, must be added during preparation.

Concentrated fish stock

• Fish concentrate is, to the preparation of fish sauces, what stock is to meat. There are many excellent ones on sale, and this can eliminate what amounts to a very fiddly preparation (we must add that fish stock which is prepared on a small-scale produces a very strong and unpleasant odour if it is not used almost immediately after it has been made).

• By way of information, and for the extremely keen and conscientious amateur, here is the recipe. Use scraps of fish (backbones, heads etc.); wash and dry them prior to grinding them. Take a 1.5 to 2 litre saucepan. Melt 30 g of butter and immediately add 1 thinly sliced discs of carrot, 1 onion, also thinly sliced, and 1 clove. Leave to cook for several minutes without browning; add dry white wine and water in equal quantities. Add parsley, thyme, bay, several peppercorns and a pinch of coarse salt. Bring to the boil and skim carefully.

• Boil vigorously, half covered, for 30 to 40 minutes. Put through a conical strainer and set aside.

ENTRÉES

In the tradition of French cookery, a meal is always made up of a main dish which is preceded by an entrée and followed by cheese or dessert. Some entrées constitute a main dish on their own (if so, then the real entrée must be lighter or easier to prepare).

In simple terms, entrées can be classified in several groups:
• soups, both hot and cold;
• meat, fish or vegetable terrines;
• a few dishes which use eggs (hot or cold) as a basic ingredient (the recipes for which will be given in the chapter on eggs);
• a few dishes, some of which are very complicated, and others which are more complicated still, and are regrouped into various hot and cold entrées;
• two individual sections will be dedicated to recipes using, on the one hand, snails and frogs, and on the other, foie gras;
• finally, salads.

SOUPS

Pumpkin soup

Preparation and cooking time
ABOUT AN HOUR AND A HALF
Ingredients
1 PUMPKIN,
550 G OF POTATOES,
150 G OF CREAM,
100 G OF GRATED CHEESE,
SOME SMALL PIECES OF TOASTED BREAD,
NUTMEG,
ALLSPICE.

• This soup is very attractive to serve since it must, in fact, be served from the pumpkin itself, and this is guaranteed to invoke a festive atmosphere.

• Cut a large circle out of the top of the pumpkin (a pumpkin weighs around 3 kg) and remove it. Take out the seeds from the inside of the pumpkin with a spoon. Scoop out the flesh taking care not to pierce the skin.

• Take about half of this flesh (the other half can be used for a gratin dish), cut it into small pieces and place in a saucepan along with 500 g of potatoes which have been peeled and cut into pieces and with 2 litres of water. Cook over a low heat for 45 minutes. Make into a purée using a vegetable grinder or a mixer. Add 150 g of cream, 100 g of grated cheese (gruyère, comté). Put the whole lot back into the pumpkin and mix together. Place in a hot oven (around 210° or gas mark 7) for 15 minutes. Serve in the pumpkin, adding a dozen or so small pieces of toasted bread at the last moment.

• **Caution:** season to taste, prior to putting the mixture back in the pumpkin. This vegetable is fairly flavourless and so, in addition to pepper, you should add a spice (nutmeg or allspice) of your choice instead of salt which, in general, we do not advise you to use.

Cabbage soup

"Thin" cabbage soup
Preparation and cooking time
ABOUT ONE AND A HALF HOURS
Ingredients
1 WHITE OR GREEN CABBAGE,
STALE SLICED BREAD,
220 G OR GRUYÈRE, CANTAL OR ROQUEFORT,
STOCK

"Thick" cabbage soup
Preparation and cooking time
ABOUT ONE AND A HALF HOURS
Ingredients
1 WHITE OR GREEN CABBAGE,
200 G OF FRESH LOIN OF PORK,
200 G OF HAM, 300 G OF ONIONS,
DUCK FAT,
550G OF SAUERKRAUT,
TINNED TOMATO PURÉE,
STOCK, 400 G OF CRÈME FRAÎCHE.

• There are several recipes for this dish. We give two of them, one of which could be called the "thin" version and the other the "thick" version.

• For the first version: blanch the leaves of a cabbage (about 800 g). Place the cabbage leaves, the slices of stale bread and the slivers of cheese (gruyère, cantal or roquefort depending on how strongly seasoned you like your soup to be) in successive layers, in an ovenproof earthenware dish. Alternate the layers so that the final layer is cheese. Add 2 litres of stock (made with stock cubes), so that all the layers are covered. Cook in a low oven for about 1 hour or until the top is browned.

• The second version is more complicated but gives a more substantial soup which can serve as a real cold weather dish.

• Blanch the cabbage and chop coarsely. Cut 200 g of pork (loin) and 200 g of ham into small squares. Brown rapidly in some butter (lard or duck fat are preferable) with 300 g of onions which have also been cut into small squares.

• Place the meat, onions and cabbage, along with 500 g of cooked sauerkraut, a small tin

Cabbage soup

of tomato purée and 1.5 litres of stock in a large casserole pot (with a lid). Bring to the boil and simmer over a low heat for 1 hour. Add the crème fraîche (400 g) just before serving.

ONION SOUP

• Slice 250 g of onions and gently cook them in butter until they are golden in colour. Sprinkle with 50 g of flour, allow to brown and then add 1 litre of stock and leave to cook for 10 minutes. Place the soup in individual ovenproof bowls. Put 2 or 3 croûtons into each one and cover generously with grated cheese. Leave to brown in the oven.

ONION AND GARLIC SOUP

• This soup, which originates in the south west of France, is extremely ancient, since it appears in cookery books as early as the XVII th century. There are regional variations but the recipe that we have chosen is as follows.

Preparation and cooking time
30 MINUTES
Ingredients
250 G OF ONIONS, 20 G OF BUTTER,
50 G OF FLOUR,
STOCK, CROÛTONS MADE WITH STALE BREAD,
100 G OF GRATED CHEESE

Preparation and cooking time
45 MINUTES
Ingredients
400 G OF ONIONS, 100 G OF GARLIC,
2 TABLESPOONS OF GOOSE GREASE OR DUCK FAT,
2 EGGS,
1 TABLESPOON OF WINE VINEGAR,
SEVERAL SLICES OF BREAD

• Finely chop 400 g of onions and 100 g of garlic. Melt the goose grease or duck fat in a casserole pot, throw in the onions and garlic so that they turn golden brown (but do not burn). Pour in 2 litres of water, put the lid on and allow to boil gently for 20 minutes. Break 2 eggs into a bowl and mix in 1 tablespoon of wine vinegar whilst beating vigorously.

• Put several slices of farmhouse loaf in a soup tureen and pour some stock over the top, leaving the bread to soak for 5 minutes. Add the eggs which have been beaten together with the vinegar, whilst gently. Serve.

• What are the variations? In Bordeaux, lard and no garlic; in Perigord, add tomato purée; in the Quercy region, radishes replace the onions.

COLD CUCUMBER SOUP

Preparation and cooking time
2 HOURS
Ingredients for 2 people:
1 CUCUMBER, SALT,
LEMON JUICE, 2 CLOVES OF GARLIC,
4 NATURAL YOGHURTS, CHIVES AND PAPRIKA.

• Peel a cucumber, cut it in two, lengthwise, and remove the seeds. Cut each part into small cubes which must be placed in a soup plate with salt to sweat for 1 hour. Drain. Place the pieces of cucumber in a soup tureen; add the lemon juice 2 peeled cloves of garlic and 4 yoghurts. Stir and leave in a cool place for 1 hour.

• Sprinkle with chives and, if required, with paprika to give more taste.

TERRINES

The main thing when preparing a terrine is to remember that it should be cooked using a bain-marie. The most famous terrines, and those that we see most often, are meat terrines but vegetables and fish can be used equally as well as a base ingredient. Some terrines are eaten warm or hot but the great majority are served cold.

FISH TERRINES

ESCABECHE SARDINES

Preparation and cooking time
45 MINUTES (+ 2 OR 3 DAYS
IN THE LARDER PRIOR TO EATING)
Ingredients
500 G OF SARDINES, 30 CL OF WHITE VINEGAR,
BAY, THYME, PEPPER, SALT, CHILLI PEPPER,
1 ONION, 1 CLOVE OF GARLIC

• This is a terrine which does not need to be cooked, which is far less of a worry for the cook (but not far less work as the sardines must be scaled, gutted, have their heads and tails cut off and then be washed and dried).

• Prepare the sardines as above and cook in a frying pan. Next, place them in an earthenware dish deep enough for them to be covered in a marinade. For 500 g of sardines you need 30 cl of white vinegar and 20 cl of water, 1 bay leaf, 1 sprig of thyme, 1 clove of garlic, pepper and salt, the tip of 1 red chilli pepper, 1 chopped onion. This marinade should be heated in the frying pan and reduced.

• Next, pour the marinade into the terrine and set aside in a cool place for 2 to 3 days prior to serving.

SOLE TERRINE
(OR DAB FISH TERRINE, DEPENDING ON YOUR TASTES AND YOUR POCKET)

• Fillet the fish in order to obtain about 800 g of flesh. Finely chop 10 tablespoons of parsley; add pepper, allspice and a little butter and mix them all together.

• Grease the bottom and the sides of a terrine liberally with butter. Place in it firstly a layer of filleted fish, then a layer of the chopped up mixture prepared as above, and so on for subsequent layers.

Preparation and cooking time
ABOUT 1 HOUR
Ingredients
800 G OF FILLET OF SOLE OR DAB FISH,
1 LARGE BUNCH OF PARSLEY, PEPPER, ALLSPICE,
1 TABLESPOON OF BUTTER

Sole terrine

• Place the terrine, with the lid on, into a bain-marie and put it in the oven (20 minutes at gas mark 6 or 7)

• Prior to serving, remove the excess butter which has come to the surface.

VEGETABLE TERRINES

Wild mushroom terrine

Preparation and cooking time
1 HOUR + THE TIME SET ASIDE IN THE REFRIGERATOR
Ingredients
500 G OF JACKET POTATOES,
500 G OF BUTTON MUSHROOMS,
LEMON JUICE,
THE EQUIVALENT OF 2 LARGE BOWLS OF MAYONNAISE.

• Cook 500 g of potatoes in their jackets. Wash and slice 500 g of button mushrooms allow them to sweat by heating them. Leave them to cool. Peel the potatoes, cut into round slices and soak for 15 minutes in the lemon juice. Make a mayonnaise.

• Take a terrine and fill as follows: one layer of potatoes, one layer of mushrooms, one layer of mayonnaise etc. Finish with a layer of mayonnaise.

• Put the terrine in the refrigerator. Serve chilled..

Courgette terrine

Preparation and cooking time
1 HOUR AND A HALF
(PLUS COOLING TIME)
Ingredients
1 KG OF COURGETTES,
200 G OF ONIONS, 2 EGGS,
2 TABLESPOONS OF CREAM,
150 G OF GRATED CHEESE,
FRESH MINT.

• Cut the courgettes into round slices (leave the skin on). Simmer and braise these slices of courgette, along with the sliced onion, in the oil over a low light. Coarsely break up the courgettes.

• Beat 2 eggs in a bowl as for an omelette. Add 2 tablespoons of cream, 6 to 8 spoonfuls of grated cheese. Mix together with the courgettes, away from the heat.

• Add the chopped herbs for seasoning (e.g. fresh mint). Pour the whole lot into a terrine and heat in a bain-marie in the oven, with the lid on, for about 1 hour.

• Leave to cool fully and then serve.

Leek quiche

Preparation and cooking time
ABOUT 1 HOUR AND A HALF
(+ COOLING TIME)
Ingredients
300 G OF LEEKS, SALT, PEPPER,
A LARGE CUP OF BÉCHAMEL SAUCE,
2 TABLESPOONS OF CREAM,
100 G OF GRATED CHEESE, 4 EGGS

• Use only the white part and the tender green part of 300 g of leeks. Cut into very thin slices. Wash and drain.

• Brown the leeks in some butter, in a frying pan, over a medium heat, for 5 to 10 minutes. Add a glass of water, salt and pepper, cover and simmer for 20 minutes stirring frequently.

• Prepare a strongly seasoned Béchamel sauce. Add the crème fraîche (2 tablespoons); grate the cheese. Break 4 eggs and beat as for an omelette.

- Add the sauce, the cheese and the eggs to the leeks, mix thoroughly away from the heat.

- Pour the mixture into a terrine after having greased the bottom and the sides with butter.

- Cook in a bain-marie for 30 minutes covered with aluminium foil.

- Serve cold.

MEAT TERRINES

RABBIT TERRINE A LA BERRICHONNE

- Heat a court bouillon: dry white wine, salt, pepper, spices, onions, carrots.
the white of an egg, in order to clarify it.

- Plunge a whole rabbit (without the liver and kidneys) and a calf's foot cut in two, into the court bouillon. Cook for 1 hour. Take out the pieces of rabbit; remove all the bones. Throw the calf's foot away.

Preparation and cooking time
ABOUT AN HOUR AND A HALF
(+ COOLING TIME
AND TIME STORED IN THE REFRIGERATOR)
Ingredients
1 WHOLE RABBIT, 1 CALF'S FOOT,
4 MEDIUM SIZED CARROTS, 5 ONIONS,
1 LITRE OF DRY WHITE WINE,
SALT, PEPPER, VARIOUS SPICES

Rabbit terrine a la berrichonne

• Put the bits of meat into a terrine. Pack it well. Pass the cooking juices through a conical strainer. Cover the pieces of meat with this juice.

• Leave to cool and place in the refrigerator.

HAM WITH PARSLEY

Preparation and cooking time
4 HOURS
(+ SOAKING TIME, COOLING TIME AND TIME STORED IN THE REFRIGERATOR)
Ingredients
1 SLIGHTLY SALTED HAM (2.5 TO 3 KG),
2 CALF'S FEET,
1 BOTTLE OF DRY WHITE WINE,
1 LARGE BUNCH OF PARSLEY,
HERBS FOR SEASONING,
3 SHALLOTS,
THE WHITE OF 1 EGG

• Soak a slightly salted ham (2.5 to 3 kg) overnight; blanch for an hour and then rinse.

• Cook for 2 hours or so with 2 calf's feet which have been cut in half lengthwise, tarragon, chervil, shallots, pepper, water and dry white wine (e.g. a bottle of light Chablis).

• Wait until the flesh can be broken up with a fork.

• After cooking, remove the bone. Mix together the fatty and the lean meat and press into a terrine.

• Put the cooking water through a conical strainer, after having brought it to the boil with the white of an egg, in order to clarify it.

• Pour the jelly into the terrine. Add a large glass of parsley which has been cut up with scissors. Mix together. Place in the refrigerator and serve chilled.

SMALL RAMEKINS OF CHICKEN LIVER PATE WITH LEEKS - (FOR 2 PEOPLE)

Preparation and cooking time
ABOUT 30 MINUTES
(+ COOLING TIME AND TIME STORED IN THE REFRIGERATOR)
Ingredients
4 SMALL LEEKS,
50 G OF BUTTER,
120 G OF CHICKEN LIVERS,
VINAIGRETTE SAUCE

• This terrine has one great advantage in that it can be served in individual dishes.

• Remove the dark green part of 4 small leeks; wash and cut the remainder en julienne. Heat 50 g of butter in a saucepan over a very low light (very low so that the butter does not "turn to oil").

• Add the pieces of leek and cook for 10 minutes. Mince 120 g of chicken livers (removing fatty and stringy parts); mix with the leeks and cook for 5 to 10 minutes. Place in 2 ramekins and leave in the refrigerator.

• When ready to serve, turn out of the ramekins and serve with a well seasoned vinaigrette.

CHICKEN LIVER PATE

• Soak 1 kg of chicken livers in iced water for 2 hours (**caution**: remove the hearts which are usually sold with the livers, and as many fatty tissues and sinews as possible). Drain and sponge dry.

• Season with pepper and leave to soak for 1 hour in 2 tablespoons of oil and 2 spoonfuls of cognac.

• Cook the whole thing in a bain-marie for 45 minutes. Drain off the liquid whilst retaining the pan in which the meat has been cooked.

• Put the cooked livers through a conical strainer (this is a delicate operation because some of the sinews are still remaining and tend to block the holes in the mesh of the strainer).

• Melt about 200 g of butter in a saucepan (still in a bain-marie), but do not allow the fat and the water to separate (watch the temperature carefully).

• Gradually mix together the chicken liver purée and the butter, over the heat, so as to obtain a smooth kind of cream.

• Pour into a terrine. Allow to cool and place in a refrigerator.

Preparation and cooking time
5 HOURS IN TOTAL
Ingredients
1 KG OF CHICKEN LIVERS,
2 TABLESPOONS OF OLIVE OIL,
2 TABLESPOONS OF COGNAC,
200 G OF BUTTER

Small ramekins of chicken liver pâté with leeks

Now we are going to suggest several different types of entrée, some of which, as we said earlier, can serve as main dishes. If serving as a main course then the quantities should be increased according to the anticipated appetite of the guests. These recipes have been grouped according to the manner in which the dish should be served, e.g. hot or cold.

VARIOUS COLD ENTRÉES

SEA FOOD PLATTER

• This dish does not require long or skilled preparation but does require careful choosing when it comes to buying the various ingredients for the platter. The composition varies according to taste (a variety of produce is essential) and the proportions vary according to appetite. For information purposes, the quantities given are for 1 person.
— 6 oysters
— 6 carpet shells;
— 1 handful of cooked winkles;
— 3 cooked langoustines;
— 1/2 cooked crab;
— 4 cooked whelks.

• Cooking:
— Winkles: after washing in a great deal of water, place them in a saucepan of cold water, bring to the boil, remove the juice immediately and set aside for 2 minutes.
— Whelks: same technique but leave to boil for 5 to 10 minutes.
— Langoustines: plunge them into boiling water with vinegar added to it (1 teaspoon to 2 litres of water). Bring back to the boil, drain straight away or, if they are large, leave them in the cooking water, away from the heat, for 2 minutes (**caution**: this is the procedure for quantities less than 1 kg so as to avoid overcooking when brought back to the boil).
— Crab: plunge them into boiling water and vinegar (1 tablespoon to 2 litres of water). Bring back to the boil and leave to boil for 15 to 25 minutes depending on the size.

• Accompanying sauces should be prepared beforehand: mayonnaise, vinegar with shallots or simply some lemon juice and powdered pepper.

OYSTER CONSOMME

Preparation and cooking time
JUST OVER AN HOUR
Ingredients
4 OYSTERS PER PERSON,
1 LARGE ONION, 1 CARROT,
1 BOUQUET GARNI, 1 TOMATO,
1 HALF-BOTTLE OF DRY WHITE WINE

• Prepare a court bouillon with 1 onion cut into thin strips, 1 carrot, also cut into pieces, 1 bouquet garni, 1 tomato, some water, of course, but, in particular, the water from the oysters which have been taken out of their shells (you can open oysters by putting them in a microwave on medium power for a few moments).

• Cook this court bouillon for 45 minutes and then strain to remove any solids. Return to the heat and add some white wine (e.g. Muscadet) - 3 or 4 glasses according to the

Oyster consomme

number of guests. When the liquid "quivers", pour in the oysters. Leave to simmer for about 10 minutes. Pour the consommé into bowls, or into individual cups in the refrigerator as it should be served properly chilled.

VARIOUS HOT ENTRÉES

HOT SMOKED HADDOCK GALANTINE
(ÉGLEFIN, HADDOCK)

• Blanch the largest leaves of a green cabbage. Place in an ovenproof dish with a thin layer of olive oil covering the bottom, then a layer of cabbage leaves, then a layer of smoked fish (this will have been poached in butter and then cooled) and a layer of cabbage leaves. Sprinkle small squares of red pepper which have been blanched after having had their pith and seeds removed. Leave in a medium oven for about 15 minutes, covered with aluminium foil. Serve cut into vertical slices.

Preparation and cooking time
30 MINUTES
Ingredients
SEVERAL LARGE GREEN CABBAGE LEAVES,
1 TEASPOON OF OIL,
2 PORTIONS OF SMOKED FISH PER PERSON,
200 G OF RED PEPPERS

MUSSELS A LA MARINIÈRE
(OFTEN CALLED BY THEIR ABBREVIATED NAME: MOULES MARINIÈRES)

Preparation and cooking time
ABOUT 30 MINUTES
Ingredients
2 LITRES OF MUSSELS,
3 MEDIUM SIZED CARROTS,
2 ONIONS, THYME, BAY,
50 G OF BUTTER,
20 CL OF WHITE WINE, PARSLEY

• Check that the mussels are tightly closed (discard any which are open), scrape and wash them several times to remove sand and small stones.

• Heat the mussels in a saucepan with parsley, carrots cut into pieces, thyme, bay and a little butter.

• Without discarding the cooking juices, add the white wine, the rest of the butter and some more parsley to the saucepan, as soon as all the mussels are open. Cook for 3 minutes without bringing to the boil.

SCALLOPS WITHE WHITE WINE

Preparation and cooking time
30 MINUTES (NOT COUNTING THE TIME SPENT TAKING THE SCALLOPS OUT OF THEIR SHELLS)
Ingredients
3 OR 4 SCALLOPS PER PERSON DEPENDING ON APPETITE, 1 TABLESPOON OF OIL,
1 KNOB OF BUTTER, 1 SHALLOT,
50 G OF BUTTON MUSHROOMS,
1 TABLESPOON OF TOMATO PURÉE (OR, BETTER STILL, 4 TABLESPOONS OF TOMATO COULIS),
10 CL OF WHITE WINE,
1 CLOVE OF GARLIC, PARSLEY, PEPPER

• Use scallops which have already been taken out of their shells. Cut each scallop into two or three strips.

• Cut the mushrooms into thin slices (wiped rather than washed in water). Chop the garlic, the shallot and the parsley, finely. Heat the oil and the butter in a small shallow frying pan, cook the strips of scallop until they are golden and then take them out of the frying pan.

• Place the shallot in the shallow frying pan and, as soon as it becomes translucent, add the mushrooms, the tomato purée (or 'coulis') and the pepper. Pour in the white wine, mix together and turn the heat up high for several minutes. Lower the heat as soon as the liquid starts to boil and leave to simmer for a few moments. Add the garlic, the parsley and the scallops for 1 or 2 minutes. Serve very hot.

Shellfish ratatouille

SHELLFISH RATATOUILLE

• Cut 1 onion, 1 aubergine, 2 courgettes, 1 red pepper and 3 tomatoes which have already been trimmed and deseeded, into small pieces. Brown all these vegetables, except the tomatoes, in a little very hot olive oil. Drain off the oil.

• Put 5 tablespoons of water, 1 tablespoon of olive oil, 4 to 5 knobs of butter, 1 tablespoon of chopped basil, 1 crushed clove of garlic and a bouquet garni into a medium sized saucepan. Add the sautéed vegetables and the cubes of tomato.

• Cover and leave to cook on a low light for 10 minutes. When ready to serve add 3 to 5 cooked langoustine tails and 4 to 6 small pieces of raw scallop. Season with salt and pepper. Mix gently with a spoon for 1 minute. Serve in a salad bowl, straight away, just as it is.

Preparation and cooking time
20 MINUTES
Ingredients for 2 people:
3 TO 5 LANGOUSTINE TAILS,
4 TO 6 SCALLOPS,
1 AUBERGINE, 2 COURGETTES, 1 RED PEPPER,
3 TOMATOES, 1 TABLESPOON OF OLIVE OIL,
4 TO 5 KNOBS OF BUTTER,
4 LEAVES OF BASIL, 1 CLOVE OF GARLIC,
1 BOUQUET GARNI,
SALT, PEPPER

LANGOUSTINE IN CABBAGE LEAF PARCELS

• This recipe, which appears to be very much to modern tastes, does, in fact, date back to the end of the XVI the century in Italy.

• Blanch the green cabbage and once it has cooled select the tenderest leaves. Take the pre-cooked langoustines or crayfish and shell them, reckoning on 3 per guest. Wrap each one in a cabbage leaf, if possible without the spine, and then wrap the whole thing in thinly sliced Parma ham. Place in an ovenproof dish.

• Prepare a tomato sauce (chopped onions, deseeded and skinned tomatoes, pepper and, most importantly, olive oil). Add the "scraps" from the pieces of Parma ham used earlier, to the sauce, chopping them finely. Pour this sauce over the "little cabbage parcels" and put in the oven for 5 to 7 minutes.

Preparation and cooking time
ABOUT 45 MINUTES
Ingredients
1 GREEN CABBAGE,
3 LANGOUSTINES OR CRAYFISH PER PERSON,
1 SLICE OF PARMA HAM
FOR 3 LANGOUSTINES,
6 ONIONS, 3 LARGE TOMATOES,
PEPPER, 3 TABLESPOONS OF OLIVE OIL

OLD STYLE SALMAGUNDI

• This recipe, which requires quite a long preparation time because of the various ingredients used, is actually fairly easy. It is taken from an XVIII century cookery book but has been adapted.

• This dish must be served in individual bowls, each of which must be deep enough to contain:
— some strips of lamb's kidneys which have been sealed over a very high heat, without any fat.
— 2 large peeled shrimps,
— some pieces of calf's sweetbread or brains (see under the heading "Offal" for how to prepare them),
— 2 oysters (removed from their shells, of course, but retaining their juice),
— 3 raw scallops, cut into strips if rather thick. Also add the red part of the scallop, but leave it whole.

Preparation and cooking time
PREPARATION IS TIME CONSUMING
AND MUST BE CARRIED AT SEPARATE TIMES
SINCE DOING THE WHOLE LOT AT ONCE,
OR DOING ONE THING AFTER ANOTHER,
IS VERY DIFFICULT UNLESS YOU HAVE SOME HELP
Ingredients for 4 people:
1 LAMB'S KIDNEY,
8 LARGE SHRIMPS,
HALF OF THE "APPLE" OF A CALF'S SWEETBREAD,
8 OYSTERS, 12 SCALLOPS,
1 LITRE OF FISH STOCK

• Bring a fish stock (excellent bottled varieties are now available) to the boil and then pour 2 ladlefuls of the stock into each bowl. The time it takes to pass from oven to table is enough to poach the oysters and the scallops. Season to taste (but do not over season so that each ingredient retains its own flavour).

SNAILS AND FROGS

Snails may be eaten other than in their shells (if they are served in their shells then obviously no preparation is necessary, they just have to be put in the oven for a while), as can be seen from the two recipes which follow.

POTTED SNAILS

Preparation and cooking time
15 MINUTES (NOT COUNTING THE TIME TAKEN FOR SOAKING THE ANCHOVIES)
Ingredients for 4 people:
8 ANCHOVY FILLETS, 24 LARGE SNAILS
(48 SMALL ONES OR 32 MEDIUM SIZED ONES),
1 TOMATO,
30 CL OF DRY WHITE WINE,
100 G OF CRÈME FRAÎCHE,
2 CLOVES OF GARLIC,
2 ONIONS

• Slightly brown the garlic and the chopped onion in the olive oil. Add 1 chopped tomato and some chopped anchovy fillets (soaked in warm water beforehand to remove the salt) and finally a little dry white wine.

• Pour the tinned snails into this sauce. Leave to simmer for 5 minutes adding the crème fraîche half way through. Season with pepper. Serve with the sauce.

Potted snails

FRICASSEED FROG'S LEGS WITH SNAILS

• Place the frog's legs in some milk and then in some flour. Sauté them in butter and add some garlic purée.

• Drain and reheat the contents of a tin of snails. Add some white wine and some herbs to season.

• Pour the whole lot into the shallow frying pan containing the frog's legs. Mix together and pour into a dish. Sprinkle with parsley.

Preparation and cooking time
15 MINUTES
Ingredients for 4 people:
24 FROGS, 24 LARGE SNAILS,
25 CL OF MILK, 4 TABLESPOONS OF FLOUR,
50 G OF BUTTER, GARLIC PURÉE,
20 CL OF DRY WHITE WINE,
6 SPRIGS OF PARSLEY

FROG'S LEGS AU GRATIN

• Soak the frog's legs in milk (count on 6 to 10 pairs of legs per person). Drain and lightly cover in flour (so that they do not stick in the frying pan). Brown in hot butter (but do not let them turn nutty brown before the frog's legs have been added). Add 2 or 3 shallots and 2 cloves of garlic chopped up together. Leave to brown, drain and place in a gratin dish.

• Prepare a large cup of parsley, chervil and chives, all cut up with scissors. Mix together with these herbs - 4 tablespoons of cream, 2 egg yolks and a little grated cheese.

• Add a large glass of white wine to the residue left in the frying pan. Add the juice of one lemon and add to the earlier mixture. Pour over the frog's legs. Cook "au gratin" in a hot oven.

Preparation and cooking time
ABOUT 45 MINUTES
Ingredients for 4 people:
24 FROGS, 25 CL OF MILK,
4 TABLESPOONS OF FLOUR, 50 G OF BUTTER,
2 OR 3 SHALLOTS, 2 CLOVES OF GARLIC,
6 SPRIGS OF PARSLEY AND THE SAME OF CHERVIL
AND CHIVES, 4 TABLESPOONS OF CREAM,
2 EGG YOLKS,
4 TABLESPOONS OF GRATED CHEESE,
1 LARGE GLASS OF WHITE WINE, 1 LEMON

FOIE GRAS

This marvellous product has a hallowed and glorious reputation which, in many people's eyes, makes it difficult to prepare; well it isn't, as you will see. In addition, you can save a great deal of money by buying foie gras uncooked and preparing it to be served hot (making foie gras in a terrine is more difficult).

Clearly we are talking here about whole duck or geese livers; we prefer the former since they seem to be "tastier" and easier to work with. It is as well to say, when you buy the liver, that you want to cut it into thin slices. Caution: one liver is made up of two lobes which are joined together by a small network of bloody muscle tissue which needs to be removed. Thin slices or cubes can only be cut by working on one lobe at a time.

Here are four recipes which, although simple, will give you and your guests a great deal of pleasure. A duck liver weighs about 500 g and you must count on using 50 g per person.

HOT FOIE GRAS WITH POTATOES

Preparation and cooking time
20 MINUTES
Ingredients
COUNT ON 50 G OF RAW FOIE GRAS PER PERSON
AND 100 G OF POTATOES,
PEPPER

• Cut one lobe of liver into cubes. Store the cubes in the refrigerator until ready to use. Sauté the "scraps" (small pieces which break off when the liver is cut up) until they are golden brown along with the peeled and cubed (the same size as the foie gras) potatoes (pre-cooked in their jackets). Add the cubes of foie gras and a little pepper. Leave to cook in the frying pan,with a lid on, for several minutes, then shake the pan to turn the whole lot over. Leave for another few minutes and serve in a very hot dish.

ESCALOPE OF FOIE GRAS RICHELIEU

Preparation and cooking time
10 MINUTES
Ingredients
COUNT ON 50 G OF RAW FOIE GRAS PER PERSON,
2 TEASPOONS OF BUTTER, 1 EGG,
A LITTLE FLOUR, SOME BREADCRUMBS,
SALT AND PEPPER, SOME PIECES OF TRUFFLE

• Cut the liver into fairly thick slices, otherwise they will break up. Put them into a dish containing a beaten egg seasoned with salt and pepper. Next transfer them to the flour and finally into the breadcrumbs.

• Heat a knob of butter in a frying pan. When the butter is hot, put in the escalopes. Leave to cook for 4 minutes on each side. Take the escalopes out and place them in a very hot dish.

**Hot foie gras
with potatoes**

• Add the pieces of truffle to the frying pan along with a drop of alcohol and a little butter. Put the whole lot into the dish in order to "coat" the escalopes.

HOT CASSEROLE OF FOIE GRAS WITH VEGETABLES

• This recipe can be made with chicory or with leeks but the technique is the same. In both cases leave the raw chicory, which has been dismantled leaf by leaf (without the hard part), or the leeks, cut into small thin slices, to "sweat" in a covered casserole dish over a low light, with some port until they are fully cooked.

• Next place the whole liver, or one lobe of it (depending on the number of guests), on top of these vegetables, after having been coated with pepper or with allspice. Leave to simmer, with the lid on, on a medium heat for 7 to 8 minutes. Serve in the casserole dish itself, cutting the portions in front of the guests.

Preparation and cooking time
15 MINUTES
Ingredients
SAME QUANTITIES AS ABOVE FOR THE FOIE GRAS,
2 WHOLE CHICORY PER PERSON
OR THE EQUIVALENT OF 6 TO 8 TABLESPOONS
OF LEEKS EN JULIENNE,
1 LARGE GLASS OF PORT, PEPPER, ALLSPICE.

HOT FOIE GRAS WRAPPED IN CABBAGE LEAVES

• Blanch the cabbage leaves. Roll up each escalope of foie gras, coated in pepper or allspice, in a cabbage leaf. Place them into a casserole pot, with a lid on, for 5 to 8 minutes with a little port. Serve in a very hot dish.

Preparation and cooking time
15 TO 20 MINUTES
(+ THE TIME TO BLANCH THE CABBAGE)
Ingredients
STILL THE SAME QUANTITIES FOR THE LIVER,
AS MANY CABBAGE LEAVES AS THERE ARE GUESTS,
1 SMALL GLASS OF PORT, PEPPER, ALLSPICE

SALADS

HOT SAUSAGE AND POTATO SALAD

• In order to be successful with this dish you need to be brave as, at one point during the recipe, you have to peel boiling potatoes.

• Cook the firm fleshed potatoes in their jackets in some water. Meanwhile, poach (15 to 20 minutes of very gentle simmering) a Morteau type sausage in some white wine. Also prepare some olive oil, the onion cut into thin slices and some pepper in a salad bowl. Peel the hot potatoes and cut into fairly thick round slices. Pour some white wine instead of vinegar over them, mix and place the rather thickly cut slices of hot sausage on top of the salad. Serve immediately.

Preparation and cooking time
ABOUT 30 MINUTES
Ingredients for 4 people:
500 G OF POTATOES,
1 LARGE MORTEAU SAUSAGE,
1 BOTTLE OF DRY WHITE WINE,
1 LARGE ONION, PEPPER,
OLIVE OIL

FENNEL SALAD

• Fennel can be eaten raw, coarsely chopped, or can be cooked (this is less well known). Fennel needs to be cooked for about 30 minutes in water and then thoroughly drained. In both cases prepare a vinaigrette dressing.

Preparation and cooking time
10 OR 40 MINUTES (DEPENDING ON WHETHER
THE FENNEL IS EATEN RAW OR COOKED)

MUSHROOM SALAD WITH CHERVIL

Preparation and cooking time
10 MINUTES
Ingredients
500 G OF BUTTON MUSHROOMS,
3 TABLESPOONS OF CRÈME FRAÎCHE,
1 LEMON, 1 BUNCH OF CHERVIL, PEPPER

• Clean and thinly slice 500 g of button mushrooms. Mix 3 tablespoons of crème fraîche, the juice of 1 lemon, 1 bunch of chervil which has been cut up using scissors, a little pepper (a striking example of how the use of salt can be avoided) together with the button mushrooms in a salad bowl. Serve chilled.

MUSHROOMS À LA MANIÈRE

Preparation and cooking time
15 MINUTES

• This is the only recipe in this book which makes reference to a very great chef. It is an homage to Manière who disappeared several years ago but who was truly inspired. Here is the recipe that he created, just as he told it to me.

• You must count on 100 g of button mushrooms per person, 2 lemons, 1 teaspoon of strong mustard, 1 egg yolk, some neutral flavoured oil (ground-nut or sunflower), salt, pepper, 1 tablespoon of ketchup, 1/2 teaspoon of Worcester sauce and 1 packet of chives.

**Mushrooms
à la Manière**

• After having cut off the stalks of the mushrooms and scraped the tops, wash them thoroughly in water, dry them and cut them into strips,widthwise, as finely as possible. Squeeze the juice of a lemon over them.

• Next make a mayonnaise by mixing together the egg yolk and the mustard and gradually adding the oil while beating.

•When the mayonnaise is done, season with salt, add the juice of the other lemon, the ketchup, the Worcester sauce, the finely chopped chives and the pepper. Mushrooms, when they are seasoned in this way, have just enough of a "kick" to whet the appetite, but retain their own flavour which is very delicate.

COURGETTES WITH MINT

• Blanch the courgettes which have been sliced into medium sized rounds (too thin and they might break up, too thick and they will not be cooked well enough) for 10 minutes, after having completely removed the stalk. As soon as they are blanched, transfer them to an open frying pan on a very high heat for 10 minutes. Take care that they do not brown, use olive oil.

• Leave to cool in a salad bowl and add mint which has been cut up with scissors. Serve chilled.

Preparation and cooking time
ABOUT 30 MINUTES
(+ COOLING TIME)
Ingredients for 4 people:
500 G OF COURGETTES, 3 TABLESPOONS OF OLIVE OIL, 2 FRESH LEAVES OF MINT

WARM COURGETTES
WITH POPPY SEEDS OR DILL

• Blanch the courgettes as above but then immediately drizzle them with olive oil and then sprinkle them with poppy seeds or dill. Serve warm.

PICKLED BEETROOT WITH NUTS

• Get hold of raw beetroot (**why?** because the industrial method of cooking beetroot, in water, removes a lot of their flavour). Cook the beetroot, individually wrapped in aluminium foil, in the oven for a good hour (cook a chicken or a leg of mutton at the same time in order to make the most of the cooking time).

• Prepare a marinade: 2 or 3 glasses of wine vinegar, the same of water, peppercorns (a dozen or so), 1 clove, some sage, some bay and a little sugar. Bring to the boil for several minutes and then leave to cool.

• Peel the beetroot and cut into pieces. Put them into a jar with the cold marinade and store the jar in a cold, dry place.

• When ready to use, cut the beetroot, taken from the jar, into very small pieces. Grind some nuts (twenty or so green walnuts, i.e. the edible part), 2 cloves of garlic. Water down with 1 or 2 tablespoons of marinade. Mix the whole lot thoroughly.

EGGS

How can you tell how fresh an egg is?
• by looking at it: the fresher the egg the more the yolk is centred in the shell;
• by plunging it into a container full of very salty water; if the egg touches the bottom, it is fresh, if, on the other hand, it floats, then its freshness is limited;
• by breaking it, the older the egg, the more liquid the white and the more it spreads out.

As a rule, an egg stays fresh for about twenty days but, however, you must be careful not to contaminate other foods in general, by bringing them into contact with the eggshells which can comprise some dangerous elements.

Eggs, when used for cold entrées, are poached or hard boiled and so it is necessary to be aware of exactly how to prepare them in this way.

For hard boiled eggs:
• Choose a receptacle which is taller rather than wider so that the eggs can be fully immersed in it. It is best to put the eggs in a small strainer (this makes it easier to get them out again after cooking).

• Bring the water (unsalted) to the boil, plunge in the eggs, wait until the water reboils and then time for 8 or 9 minutes according to the size of the eggs. Take out the eggs and plunge them into cold water (this will eliminate the layer of steam between the egg and its shell). Peel them. Caution: if you put the eggs in before the water is boiled the yolk will shift to one side of the shell where the white will be at its most fragile if you remove the yolk as described later on.

To get poached eggs:
• Proceed as follows - this is not as easy as many people think. Choose a receptacle which is clearly taller, rather than wider. Fill it right to the top and add a little salt, 1 tablespoon of vinegar (why vinegar? to contain the egg white). It is not advisable to cook more than 3 eggs at once.

• Bring the water to the boil and reduce the heat but still let the water boil gently. Break the eggs one after another into a saucer and slide them, one by one, into the pan (do not do this from a great height!). Leave for 1 and a half to 2 minutes maximum. Take the pan off the heat almost immediately, put the lid on and leave for 3 minutes.

• Next remove each egg with a skimming ladle and rinse with slow running cold water. Each egg can then be "prepared". Cut off ragged bits of egg white with scissors.

There are many recipes in which hard boiled eggs are used in cold entrées, the general principle being to vary the stuffing which is placed inside the egg with its yolk removed (gently so as not to cut into the white). In all cases, the yolk should be crumbled and incorporated into the product chosen for the stuffing and then the whole lot can be put back in the envelope provided by the white of the egg.

Mere Poulard Omelette

Hard boiled eggs stuffed with tuna

. Use tinned tuna and add mustard or paprika to enliven the flavour. Place the eggs on salad leaves.

Hard boiled eggs stuffed with salmon, with rillettes (potted meats), with anchovy paste

• Same technique.

Eggs au gratin with shrimps and paprika

• Cut 2 hard boiled eggs per person into medium sized slices and place in a dish. In a bowl mix together 10 cl of crème fraîche, 1 tablespoon of mustard and 50 g (per person) of shrimp tails which have been peeled and cut in half. Sprinkle with paprika and pour over the eggs. Add grated cheese and cook au gratin.

Hard boiled eggs stuffed à la Mireille

• The stuffing is once again made from tuna (tinned) and from concentrated tomato purée. Furthermore, the presentation is more elaborate (in particular, with regard to the colours).

Hard boiled eggs stuffed à la Mireille

Place some salad leaves and some sliced tomatoes so they cover the bottom of the serving dish. Place the stuffed eggs on top of this and surround them with black olives and anchovy fillets. Prepare a vinaigrette dressing to accompany the dish and serve chilled.

EGGS TOUPINEL

• This little known dish is not difficult to prepare. You should use large Bintje potatoes cooked in foil in the oven (after having cut out a lid out of which the flesh can later be removed). After cooking, remove as much flesh as is possible without breaking the skin.

• Mix this flesh together with some butter, some cream, a dash of nutmeg and some very small pieces of lean ham. In the bottom of each potato, place a teaspoonful of cream and a little of the purée, leaving space for one egg (yolk and white). Grate a little cheese over the top. Put in the oven so as to cook the egg.

Preparation and cooking time
20 MINUTES
Ingredients Per person:
1 EGG, 1 VERY LARGE POTATO,
1 TEASPOON OF BUTTER,
THE SAME OF CREAM,
SMALL PIECES OF LEAN HAM,
NUTMEG, GRATED CHEESE

SCRAMBLED EGGS

• So as to be sure of obtaining a smooth creamy mass, in which the white and the yolk are properly mixed together, it is preferable to use a bain marie (this is to avoid the direct contact with the heat which you would have if you used a frying pan or a saucepan).

• Beat the eggs in a bowl. Heat some water in a saucepan big enough to hold another pan. Pour the eggs into the second saucepan with some butter (2 or 3 knobs). As soon as the heat from the water begins to make the contents of the small saucepan coagulate, stir with a wooden spoon, constantly scraping the sides and the bottom of the pan. Prior to serving, add a little pepper, some tarragon cut with scissors or any other herbs and spices which you particularly like, or better still, some asparagus tips.

POACHED EGGS IN A RED WINE SAUCE

• This famous Burgundian recipe requires a great deal of care as it involves a series of different operations. It is a recipe for poached eggs in a red wine sauce, on croûtons, with onions, pieces of diced pork and mushrooms. Each egg is prepared individually (the quantities given here are for 4 eggs).

• If possible use spring onions. Blanch them for 10 minutes and, in addition, blanch the tiny pieces (about 20) of diced smoked bacon.
Prepare 20 to 25 button mushrooms by cutting them into four. Put them into a saucepan with a little water and a knob of butter and braise for 5 to 10 minutes. Rub two crusts of stale bread with cloves of garlic. All this may be prepared in advance.

• Before the meal, prepare the liquid in which the eggs are to be poached: a bottle of wine (a red burgundy or beaujolais, for example, in order to remain faithful to the region of origin of the dish) with 2 chopped shallots and 1 chopped onion, some thyme, some bay, some parsley and 1 clove of garlic. Cook the whole lot for 15 to 20 minutes. Pass the wine through a

Preparation and cooking time
1 HOUR
Ingredients for 4 eggs:
8 TO 10 WHITE SPRING ONIONS,
20 SMALL PIECES OF SMOKED BACON,
20 TO 25 SMALL BUTTON MUSHROOMS,
1 KNOB OF BUTTER,
CROÛTONS OF STALE BREAD,
2 CLOVES OF GARLIC,
1 BOTTLE OF RED WINE,
2 SHALLOTS, 1 ONION,
BAY, THYME, PARSLEY,
1 TABLESPOON OF FLOUR, 50 G OF BUTTER

strainer so as to remove any sediment and then pour it into a large saucepan and poach the eggs in it. Then remove the eggs and reduce the liquid over a medium heat (10 minutes).

• In a salad bowl, mix together 1 tablespoon of flour and 50 g of butter so as to get a sort of smooth paste. Add the onions, the pieces of bacon and the mushrooms. Pour the liquid used for poaching the eggs over the top.

• In each ramekin, or very small deep dish, place a croûton, then an egg and then sur-round with garnish and coat with the liquid (which by this stage has turned into a sauce). Season with pepper just before serving, if necessary.

« GYPSY » EGGS

• Here the base for the dish is tomato. Choose tomatoes which are quite large, parti-cularly at the base (why? so that they do not tip over during preparation or cooking). Cut off the tops, remove the flesh with a small spoon (without breaking the skin) and put into the oven for several minutes with some grains of rice inside so as to soak up the liquid.

• Break one egg into each tomato, sprinkle with grated cheese and then replace the tops. Sprinkle with a little oil and cook in a medium oven for about 10 minutes.

EGGS EN COCOTTE WITH CREAM

Eggs en cocotte with cream

• Melt a little butter (hardly any) in a small earthenware pot, in a bain-marie, and pour in 1 tablespoon of cream and 1 or two broken eggs. Bring the bain-marie to the boil and leave for 6 to 8 minutes which is when the white will cease to be liquid. Serve piping hot and season to taste.

• At the point when the mixture is poured into the pot in the bain-marie, you can add different ingredients of your choice: tarragon cut up with scissors, grilled sardine fillets, tomato coulis, mustard etc.

TRUFFLE AND EGGS

• Truffles are terribly expensive but you should be aware of one very interesting characteristic that they possess. Their odour, which is so sought after, can impregnate eggs, thanks to the permeable nature of their shells. By placing a truffle along with some uncooked eggs in a hermetically sealed container, you will get eggs which, when scrambled or even simply boiled, will taste of the truffle. These eggs can also be prepared "en cocotte".

SARDINE OMELETTE

• Fillet 4 medium sized sardines after they have been cooked in a frying pan (this is clearly much easier than filleting the raw fish). Soak for 1 hour in a little lemon juice, some pepper, some oil and a pinch of herbs (e.g. thyme or tarragon).

• Break 6 to 8 eggs, beat and pour into a hot frying pan with melted butter. Place the sardines immediately on top of the eggs whilst they are still liquid. Continue as for a "traditional" omelette. Some people eat this dish cold.

Preparation and cooking time
15 MINUTES (+ THE SOAKING TIME)
Ingredients for 4 people:
4 SARDINE FILLETS, 6 TO 8 EGGS, PEPPER, LEMON JUICE, OIL, THYME, TARRAGON, 1 TABLESPOON OF BUTTER

MERE POULARD OMELETTE

• This dish, which originates from a restaurant in Mont-Saint-Michel, has become legendary, and so, of course, there are many variations. The recipe given here is considered the most "traditional". The originality of the recipe lies in the fact that the whites and the yolks of the eggs are separated. The quantities given are for an omelette for 4 people.

• Use a frying pan with a heavy bottom (these are less common than you may think). In a salad bowl, beat the yolks of 8 eggs. In another bowl, do the same with the egg whites but without them "forming peaks".

• Melt 30 g of butter in the frying pan and as soon as it begins to sputter, pour in the eggs. In a third container, lightly whip 2 tablespoons of crème fraîche and pour this cream over the egg yolks as soon as they begin to "take". Immediately add the egg whites as well.

• This should be cooked over a high flame for about 3 minutes. The omelette can be seasoned with a mixture of chopped parsley, chervil and tarragon.

Ingredients for 4 people:
8 EGGS,
30 G OF BUTTER,
2 TABLESPOONS OF CRÈME FRAÎCHE,
PARSLEY, TARRAGON, CHERVIL

MEAT

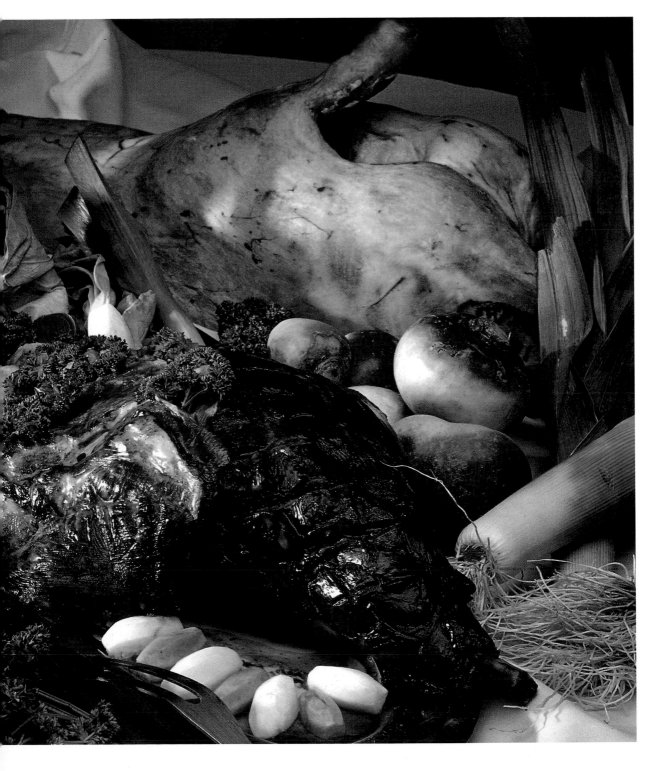

BEEF

Beef can be adapted to all types of cooking methods and is used for braising ('boeuf mode' - beef braised in red wine with vegetables, 'boeuf bourguignon' - beef stew, 'bouillon' - beef broth or stock), and above all for grilling and roasting (see below for some advice on this method of cooking).

It is interesting to note that the word "beef" should, in fact, be reserved for the castrated male of the bovine species, but, in effect, beef comes from both males (bulls) and females (cows, heifers).

GRILLED MEAT

• The basis of a grilled meat dish is the rapid coagulation of the meat's blood and proteins which prevents the meat juices from escaping. **Meat should never be salted before it is put in the frying pan** as the salt encourages the blood to flow and this, as

Fillet of beef Stroganof

it runs out onto the bottom of the frying pan, prevents the meat from sealing. On the other hand, it is good to smear the meat with oil (rather than pouring this straight into the frying pan). Allow the meat to settle at room temperature prior to cooking (to avoid the violent temperature contrast that you get when meat is used straight from the refrigerator).

• It is not the weight of a piece of beef but its thickness which should determine the cooking time. Beef should always be cooked at a hot or very hot temperature. There are four cooking stages:
— **blue:** the meat is sealed on both sides and served as soon as it is golden brown. It remains raw and cold on the inside. Its colour is reddy blue;
— **rare:** (called "vert-cuit" - i.e.' tender', by the professionals). The meat, when it is cut, is very red and bloody.
— **medium:** a pink juice flows from the meat when it is cut.
— **well done:** there is no juice at all. The meat is cooked through to the centre.

• The **château** (this is the name used by professional butchers or caterers as it avoids taking part in the chateaubriand-châteaubriant conflict) is a 3 to 5 cm thick piece of fillet. The **tournedos** is also cut from the fillet of beef but is a little less thick (2 cm) and is edged with a piece of fat which gives it its rounded shape. Nowadays it is prepared more and more frequently without the fat which adds nothing to the meat (apart from extra weight when it is sold and extra fat when it is cooked).

• After cooking a roast, take the meat out of the oven and leave for a while before carving. In this way the blood will not flow as soon as the meat is cut but will remain inside the roast.

FILLET OF BEEF STROGANOF

• Cut 600 g of fillet of beef or topside into thin strips (1/2 cm wide and 1/2 cm thick). Brown in a frying pan containing 10 cl of very hot oil for 1 minute (just enough time for the meat to change colour). Take the meat out with a skimming ladle and throw away the oil.

• Use the same frying pan to sweat 6 finely chopped shallots in 3 knobs of butter for several minutes, stirring them with a wooden spoon. Add 5 tablespoons of crème fraîche, some powdered pepper and some mild flavoured paprika (also in powdered form). Boil just for an instant and then place the meat in the sauce (with any juice that has come out of it during cooking) but only leave it long enough to reheat, left any longer the meat will become rubbery.

Preparation and cooking time
15 TO 20 MINUTES
Ingredients for 4 people:
600 G OF FILLET OF BEEF OR TOPSIDE,
2 TABLESPOONS OF OIL, 6 SHALLOTS,
3 KNOBS OF BUTTER,
5 TABLESPOONS OF CRÈME FRAÎCHE,
POWDERED PEPPER, POWDERED PAPRIKA

BEEF TIED IN STRING

• The preparation for this dish is very simple. Use a piece of fillet or topside of about 1 kg in weight (obviously without the fat). It must be compact, almost as long as it is wide, and tied up with a long piece of string part of which is hanging free.

• Use a deep cooking pot which should be filled with salted water (8 to 10 g of salt per litre of water). Bring to the boil and plunge in the meat in one go, attaching the string, for

Preparation and cooking time
40 MINUTES MAXIMUM
Ingredients
1 KG OF FILLET OF BEEF OR TOPSIDE

example, to the handle of a wooden spoon, so that the meat does not touch either the bottom or the edges of the pot.

• **Why** in boiling salted water? When meat is plunged into cold water, as, for example, with pot-au-feu (beef broth), exchanges between the water and the juices contained in the meat will occur, but if, as for "boeuf à la ficelle", the meat is plunged into cold salty water, the surface of the meat and, more precisely, the albumin, coagulates straight away creating an impermeable surface.

• Wait until the water is boiling again and leave to cook for 25 minutes so as to obtain very bloody meat. Do not worry about the greyish colour of the outside of the meat. Slice straight away and serve with a suitable sauce.

PEPPERED STEAK

Preparation and cooking time
ABOUT 15 MINUTES
Ingredients per person:
200 G TAKEN FROM THE HEART OF A FILLET OF BEEF,
PEPPERCORNS, OLIVE OIL,
3 TABLESPOONS OF CRÈME FRAÎCHE,
1 SPOONFUL OF VEAL STOCK,
1 TEASPOON OF MARC BRANDY OR CALVADOS

• This dish may seem banal, but if cooked correctly it can be particularly good.

• Cut from the fillet of beef, and more precisely from its centre, a thick piece of steak (3 cm at least). Roll the meat in coarsely ground peppercorns or "mignonette" (not powdered pepper) and oil both sides. Seal in a frying pan over a hot flame and cook according to personal preference (see the heading "grilled meat" above). Turn the meat over with a wooden spoon. Put the meat to one side.

• Add 3 tablespoons of crème fraîche and 1 spoonful of veal stock to the residue left in the frying pan. Mix together well, scraping the bottom of the frying pan with the wooden spoon. Add 1 teaspoon of marc brandy or calvados, bring to the boil and then remove from the heat immediately. Pour the sauce into a sauceboat so that it can be used to coat the meat once it is on the plate.

RIB STEAK A LA BORDELAISE

Preparation and cooking time
40 MINUTES
Ingredients for 4 people:
2 BEEF MARROW BONES,
4 X 200 G RIB STEAKS,
1 TABLESPOON OF OLIVE OIL, 100 G OF BUTTER,
1 GLASS OF RED BORDEAUX,
5 SHALLOTS, 1 LEMON,
SEVERAL SPRIGS OF PARSLEY, PEPPER

• Poach 2 beef marrow bones for 10 minutes in boiling water. Keep them hot. Reduce a glass of red Bordeaux with 5 chopped shallots and a little thyme and bay. Pass through a conical strainer and then introduce 75 g of butter and the finely chopped bone marrow over a very low light. Season with pepper and a sliver of lemon. Keep hot while you grill the steaks, brushed with olive oil. Cook according to taste.

• Meanwhile, blend a large knob of butter with a mixture of chopped shallots and parsley. Place the steaks on the serving dish topped with a little of this flavoured butter and the remains of the bone marrow cut into rounds. Serve the sauce separately.

BEEF AND CARROTS

• Choose a fairly wide, thick bottomed, casserole pot. Oil the base lightly and gently brown a piece of neck of beef (about 1,5 kg) with the fatty side facing the bottom of the pot. When the meat is golden brown on this side turn it over and after several minutes add a calf's foot which has been cut in two, lengthwise, and a beef tail cut into sections.

• Leave all that to brown for about 10 minutes, still on a low light, turning the pieces of meat. Next, take them out of the pot, throw away the fat and put the meat and bones back into the casserole. Add 2 onions which have been peeled and cut into 4 or 6 depending on their size, 4 leeks which have been washed and cut into pieces, just up to the middle of the green part, and a bouquet garni placed right in the middle. Cover with water and dry white wine (3/4 to 1/4) to about 1 cm over the top of the ingredients.

• Leave to cook very gently, with a lid on, for 2 hours.

• Then add 2.5 kg of carrots which have been peeled and cut into large rounds and cook for another hour. Taste and then season (pepper, allspice). Remove the calf's foot and serve in the cooking pot.

• It should be noted that this dish can be served cold. It will have a marrowy consistency thanks to the jelly which has come out of the calf's foot and has "set" during cooling.

BŒUF BOURGUIGNON (BOURGUIGNON BEEF)

Preparation and cooking time
ABOUT 3 HOURS
Ingredients
1.5 KG OF NECK OF BEEF,
1 CALF'S FOOT, 1 BEEF TAIL, 2 LARGE ONIONS,
4 LEEKS, 1 HALF-BOTTLE OF DRY WHITE WINE,
2.5 KG OF CARROTS, PEPPER, ALLSPICE,
5 TABLESPOONS OF OIL

Preparation and cooking time
2 HOURS (+ MARINADING TIME)
Ingredients
1.5 KG OF NECK OF BEEF,
1 MARINADE,
150 G OF SLIGHTLY SALTED BACON,
15 SMALL ONIONS, 3 TO 4 CLOVES OF GARLIC,
1 TABLESPOON OF OIL,
50 G OF BUTTER,
1 TABLESPOON OF MEAT STOCK,
70 G OF KNEADED BUTTER

Bourguignon beef

• This "stew" has the advantage that it can easily be reheated without losing any of its flavour.

• Take a piece of about 1.5 kg of neck of beef (a piece of the shoulder which is also known as the bladebone), cut off the fat and cut into pieces of approximately 50 g each. Marinade for 12 h. The marinade must entirely cover the meat.

• Starting with cold water (to remove the salt), blanch 150 g of slightly salted bacon cut into small cubes. Brown these cubes with a little butter and some small onions which have been peeled and blanched, take the whole lot out of the pot and put to one side. Place the pieces of meat, which have been thoroughly drained, into the same cooking pot and start to brown them, but then very quickly add the marinade juice, and its solid ingredients, in several parts. When the contents of the pot has been reduced by half, add 3 or 4 cloves of crushed garlic and 1 tablespoon of concentrated tomato purée. Leave to cook over a low light for 1 hour and 30 minutes. A half hour before the end of the cooking time, add the pieces of bacon and the small onions.

• Put the meat to one side. Add 1 tablespoon of meat stock and 70 g of butter which has been rubbed into flour. Quickly bring to the boil just for a few moments. Coat the meat with this sauce.

PORK

This is very much an all purpose meat, from a gastronomic point of view, you understand.
Certainly, for religious reasons as well as for reasons of local hygiene, its use is forbidden by two great religions but, when it is used, pork is used for everything, from the butcher's shop to the shop selling Moroccan leather goods and paintings, and, of course, the delicatessen. It must be cooked longer than other meats but not so as to end up with a piece of meat which is completely dried out. This is where a "trick of the trade" can come in handy: if you are using frozen meat, defrost in milk; if you are using fresh meat for a roast, blanch in boiling water for 15 to 20 minutes, depending on the size, and then roast as if the meat was still raw. By doing so, you will end up with a tender piece of meat. The slices will be pink if, prior to blanching, you have wrapped the meat, covered in salt (1 tablespoon), in aluminium foil, and left it in a cool place for 5 to 6 hours.

WHOLE OVEN ROASTED HAM

Preparation and cooking time
5 HOURS (PLUS THE TIME FOR SOAKING TO REMOVE THE SALT)
Ingredients
1 WHOLE SMOKED HAM (3 TO 4 KG)

• This is a very simple recipe and is extremely useful for a meal where there are a lot of guests.

• Use a whole smoked ham (3 to 4 kg). Soak for 24 hours to remove the salt and change the water twice. Dry and wrap in aluminium foil closed at the top (**why** at the top?

Whole oven roasted ham

so that when you take the ham out of the dish to carve it, the fat does not run out every-where).

• Place in a hot oven (gas mark 6) for at least 5 hours. Cut into fairly thick slices (ham is better when cut in thick slices, the opposite is true for roast beef).

GRILLADE OF PORK

• This piece of pork which bears the name of the manner in which it is prepared, is little known. It is, in fact, the flank or loin (of the pork).

• Seal the pork in butter over a very high flame. Turn it over (for it is always quite a small cut of meat) and leave to cook, with a lid on, over a low light for several minutes. The meat residue left in the frying pan can be diluted with a little crème fraîche. You can also add some small onions which can be browned at the same time as the meat. Blanch these small onions beforehand (**why?** because if they have been blanched they will not fall apart in the frying pan).

Preparation and cooking time
10 MINUTES
Ingredients for 4 people:
4 WHOLE PORK CHOPS,
2 TABLESPOONS OF BUTTER,
3 TABLESPOONS OF CRÈME FRAÎCHE,
15 SMALL WHITE ONIONS

SAUPIQUET MONTBARDOIS (MONTBARD SPICY STEW)

Preparation and cooking time
ABOUT 3 HOURS
(+ SOAKING TIME TO REMOVE THE SALT)
Ingredients
1 WHOLE SALTED HAM (3 TO 4 KG),
1 BOTTLE OF WHITE WINE, 3 CARROTS,
3 ONIONS, 2 LITRES OF WHITE STOCK,
2 TOMATOES, 20 SMALL WHITE ONIONS,
250 G OF TINNED PETITS POIS,
250 G OF CRÈME FRAÎCHE,
1 SMALL GLASS OF MARC (FROM BURGUNDY),
GRATED CHEESE

• This recipe has the great advantage of enabling you to use up the leftovers from the roast ham prepared as above. You can equally as well use a salted fresh ham which has been cooked twice (after being soaked to remove the salt), first in water (15 minutes per pound of meat) and then in a stew pot with carrots and onions, 1 bottle of dry white wine, some white stock (2 litres) and a bouquet garni.

• For cooking, cut the ham into thick slices. Place them in a gratin dish.

• Prepare a mixture made up of small onions which have been lightly browned in butter, button mushrooms which have been thinly sliced and sweated, 2 tomatoes which have been peeled, deseeded and coarsely chopped, 1 tin of extra fine petits pois, 250 g of crème fraîche and 1 small glass of marc (from Burgundy). Pour this mixture, which has now become fairly smooth, over the ham, sprinkle with grated cheese and leave to cook 'au gratin' in a very hot oven.

Veal saute Marengo

VEAL

The cooking of veal is a very delicate affair as the various cuts of meat all have different culinary properties.

Whatever the cut, however, cooking must be slow and temperate. Veal is a product which must be "simmered". Caution: industrial type food processing, that is to say treatment with hormones, often results in the veal being rather spongy. This means that you should try and get hold of meat from a calf which has been fed exclusively on its mother's milk (this is obviously more expensive) if you want to rediscover the traditional quality of veal.

PROVENCALE ESCALOPE OF VEAL

• The word escalope comes from the German Schale (shell) because, up until the XIX th century it was served rolled up in the shape of a shell. In general it is a thin slice of meat, but here, in contrast, we prefer to slice it thickly so that we can cook it without worrying (veal has a tendency to dry up during cooking and this is more likely to happen when the meat is cut thinly).

• If possible, the escalope (2 to 3 cm thick) should be taken from the fillet (the rear of the animal). Gently make tiny cuts in the sides of the escalope (**why?** so that the meat does not curl up into a round shape during cooking by "shrivelling up".

• Prepare a tomato fondue in some olive oil: peeled and coarsely chopped tomatoes, thinly sliced onions, some herbs (marjoram, oregano, savory), 1 tablespoon of ruby port and 1 chicken liver which has been finely diced. **Caution:** cooking must be long and slow in order to get a smooth mixture, but the tomatoes can easily "catch" in the pan.

• Place the escalopes (1 per person) in a little flour and 1 beaten egg. Brown in olive oil over a low light for 10 minutes. Place the escalopes in a ovenproof dish and cover with the tomato fondue. Leave to cook for several minutes in a hot oven (240m - gas mark 8).

Preparation and cooking time
ABOUT 30 MINUTES
Ingredients
1 THIN 200 G SLICE PER PERSON,
3 TOMATOES,
4 ONIONS,
1 CHICKEN LIVER,
2 TABLESPOONS OF OIL,
1 TABLESPOON OF RUBY PORT,
SEVERAL SPRIGS OF MARJORAM, OREGANO,
SAVORY, 1 EGG,
1 TABLESPOON OF FLOUR

VEAL SAUTE MARENGO

• This dish takes its name (or would have taken its name, for it is more of a legend than a historic fact) from the battle of Marengo (June 1800) at the outbreak of which, it was prepared by Bonaparte.

• Use 1 kg of veal cut into pieces of approximately 50 g. If possible, choose the shoulder and the breast (this joint is located in the lower part of the animal). Place them in a very large saucepan (in technical terminology a "sauteuse" - a shallow frying pan) in which the

Preparation and cooking time
ABOUT AN HOUR
Ingredients
1 KG OF SHOULDER OR BREAST OF VEAL,
3 TABLESPOONS OF OLIVE OIL,
3 ONIONS,
2 SHALLOTS, 1 CARROT,
20 CL OF DRY WHITE WINE,
6 TOMATOES, 2 CLOVES OF GARLIC,
1 BOUQUET GARNI,
2 TABLESPOONS OF CRÈME FRAÎCHE

oil has been heated. Cook for 6 to 7 minutes, just until they are golden brown, then turn them over, but under no circumstances put a fork into them (**why?** because we are aiming to keep the juice inside the meat and we do this by quickly sealing the meat, thereby preventing the blood and juices from flowing out of it).

• As soon as the meat changes colour, add 3 thinly sliced onions, 2 chopped shallots, 1 finely diced carrot. After several minutes, add 20 cl of dry white wine, in two stages, then 6 tomatoes which have been deseeded and coarsely chopped, 3 to 4 tablespoons of sauce stock, 20 cl of bouillon, 2 cloves of garlic and a bouquet garni. Leave to cook for 30 to 35 minutes, without a lid, over a medium heat. Seal the meat and put it to one side but keep it warm (in a covered dish). Break up the remaining ingredients left in the shallow frying pan, remove the bouquet garni, add 2 tablespoons of crème fraîche and then test to see if seasoning is required (this is very variable depending on the nature of the juices produced by all the different ingredients which make up the recipe). Pour the sauce over the meat.

• Legend has it that the accompaniment for this dish consisted of fried eggs, crayfish and croûtons (this is assuming that Bonaparte's cook had both the time and the ingredients at his disposal.....). Some people like to add mushrooms to the sauce.

MINCED VEAL FRICASSEED WITH ARTICHOKES AND PEAS

Preparation and cooking time
ABOUT 30 MINUTES
Ingredients for 4 people:
500 G OF CHUMP END OF LOIN OF VEAL,
1 TABLESPOON OF OIL,
5 OR 6 SHALLOTS,
1 SMALL GLASS OF WHITE WINE,
1 TABLESPOON OF MEAT STOCK,
2 ONIONS, 50 G OF BUTTER,
3 ARTICHOKE HEARTS,
1 X 250 G TIN OF PETITS POIS

• Cut 500 g of chump end of loin (a joint located right at the far end of the back, towards the tail) into small rectangles of 1 cm by 2 cm. Sauté in very hot oil for 5 minutes. During this cooking time add 5 or 6 finely chopped shallots. **Caution:** do not use too much oil; veal nowadays, if it does not come from a calf which has been fed only on its mother's milk, releases a lot of water due to the way in which the animal has been fed. Water is also released if you use frozen meat. Remove the pieces of veal with a skimming ladle and put to one side.

• Dilute the meat juices, left in the pan, with white wine (a small glass), add 1 tablespoon of meat stock and gently reduce. Add 2 thinly slice onions, 50 g of butter and beat with a whisk. Put the meat back in and add 3 artichoke hearts cut into four, a tin of petits pois. Leave these in the saucepan to heat up but do not bring to the boil.

FRICANDEAU (BRAISED VEAL)

Preparation and ingredients
ABOUT 2 HOURS
Ingredients for 4 people:
1 FILLET OF VEAL, A FEW BACON RINDS,
1/2 CALF'S FOOT, 6 CARROTS, 1 ONION,
ABOUT HALF A BOTTLE OF DRY WHITE WINE
AND THE SAME OF BOUILLON,
3 TABLESPOONS OF OLIVE OIL

• There are several recipes which go by this name and vary according to the cut of meat used. It can be a fillet of veal, cut from the knuckle, browned in a casserole pot with some oil. As soon as the meat is sealed, take it out of the pot. Garnish the bottom of the pot with several pieces of bacon rind and replace the fillet with half a calf's foot, some carrots cut into rounds and 1 onion. Add some bouillon and some dry white wine (in equal quantities) up to the top of the meat or a little below it (do not cover it completely). Bring to the boil and cook, with a lid on, for 1 hour and 30 minutes over a low light. If there is still too much liquid, let it evaporate by removing the lid. Remove the calf's foot prior to serving.

• Another recipe uses as its basic ingredient a medium sized (5 cm) slice of the topside of veal and leaves out the calf's foot.

Osso buco

• This dish is not, of course, French in origin and it has kept its Italian name. But this "empty bone" (literal translation) has become so much a part of French cuisine that we could not leave it out. The recipe takes quite a long time to prepare.

• Take quite a large shallow frying pan so that the pieces of knuckle can lie flat. Take quite a thick slice of knuckle of veal per person. **Caution:** carefully check that the bone is not hollow as the marrow, that it should contain, contributes to the success of the dish. Brown the slices in very hot oil until they are golden brown on both sides. Take them out of the pan and put to one side.

• Cut 4 or 5 turnips, 5 or 6 carrots, 1/2 celeriac, 3 or 4 large onions, 2 cloves of garlic en julienne. Add 40 to 50 g of butter. Brown over quite a high flame, turning the contents of the pan with a wooden spoon so that they do not stick. Pour in 20 cl of dry white wine,

Preparation and cooking time
1 HOUR AND A QUARTER
Ingredients
1 SLICE OF KNUCKLE OF VEAL PER PERSON,
3 TABLESPOONS OF OLIVE OIL,
4 OR 5 TURNIPS,
5 OR 6 CARROTS, 1/2 CELERIAC,
3 OR 4 LARGE ONIONS, 2 CLOVES OF GARLIC,
50 G OF BUTTER, 10 CL OF DRY WHITE WINE,
1 SMALL TIN OF TOMATO PURÉE,
1 BOUQUET GARNI

Osso buco

a small tin of concentrated tomato purée, 3 or 4 tablespoons of veal stock and a bouquet garni. Bring to the boil, stirring well. Put the slices of knuckle back in the pan and leave to cook, with a lid on, over a low light, for at least 1 hour.

• Cut some lemon and orange zest en julienne. Blanch until they become soft. Drain and add to the frying pan at the end of the cooking time.

CÔTE DE VEAU FOYOT (VEAL CHOP À LA FOYOT)

Preparation and cooking time
ABOUT 1 HOUR AND A HALF
Ingredients
1 VEAL CHOP FOR 2 PEOPLE,
300 G OF ONIONS, 150 G OF SHALLOTS,
30 CL OF DRY WHITE WINE,
THE SAME OF BOUILLON,
1 TABLESPOON OF FLOUR,
1 EGG, SOME BREADCRUMBS,
3 KNOBS OF BUTTER,
100 G OF GRATED CHEESE

• This little known dish, which is so delightful when it is successfully prepared (the secret lies in the smoothness of the mixture), takes its name from a cook from the last century. There are some variations of this recipe.

• Use very thick veal chops (it is vital that they be from a calf that has been fed exclusively on its mother's milk) together, of course, with the bones. One chop is enough for two people.

• Prepare an onion fondue: chopped shallots with white wine (30 cl) and some bouillon (the same amount). Do not stint on the number of onions and shallots and take care that this fondue is fairly liquid. Place the chop or chopsin the flour (gently), a beaten egg yolk and finally in breadcrumbs. Seal in a frying pan with some butter (we are not cooking here but merely looking for a rapid coagulation: again it is a question of keeping the juices inside the meat). This takes 5 to 7 minutes.

• Place the chop in a gratin dish. Cover it with the purée prepared earlier, this must entirely cover the meat. Cover with aluminium foil and a leave in a low oven for at least 1 hour. In the last quarter of an hour of cooking time, remove the foil and sprinkle generously with grated parmesan (**why** parmesan? because it has quite a strong taste and this means that you will not have to season later on).

Leg of lamb

Savoyarde escalope of veal

• Choose fairly thick escalopes. Brown them on both sides in some butter. Place each one on top of a slice of smoked ham in a gratin dish, put to one side but keep warm.

• Dilute the cooking juices from the escalopes with a little white wine and some crème fraîche. Simmer some finely chopped shallots in this liquid and add some mushrooms (cepes or chanterelles).

• Pour the whole lot over the escalopes. Cover with grated cheese and cook 'au gratin' in the oven.

Preparation and cooking time
About 30 minutes
Ingredients per person:
1 x 200 g escalope cut
from the chump end of loin of veal,
1 slice of smoked ham,
1 glass of dry white wine,
100 g of crème fraîche, 5 or 6 shallots,
100 g of mushrooms, 100 g of grated cheese,
1 tablespoon of butter

LAMB

When it is 14 months old, lamb becomes mutton. For the first six weeks of its life the animal is said to be a "suckling lamb", as it has not been weaned. Lamb and mutton are very fatty meats so it is a good idea to remove as much fat as possible prior to cooking and to keep the fats used in cooking to a minimum.

Leg of lamb with potatoes

• Use a leg of lamb weighing about 2 kg. Remove as much fat as is possible.

• Peel 1 kg of potatoes, not the type which "break up" during cooking, and cut them into fairly thick rounds. Place a little duck fat (or lard) in the bottom of a high-sided gratin dish and arrange the rounds of potato in layers superimposed with 10 cloves of unpeeled garlic. Pour in 50 cl of bouillon and cook for 15 minutes in a hot oven (240m - gas mark 8). Then place the meat on top. Leave to cook in a medium oven (gas mark 5) for 1 hour, turning the leg of lamb half way through the cooking time.

Preparation and cooking time
About 2 hours
Ingredients
1 kg of potatoes,
1 leg of lamb weighing 2 kg,
12 cloves of garlic,
50 cl of bouillon,
some duck fat or some lard

Lamb stew with vegetables

• There are two versions of this recipe, which differ in the accompaniment used: "printanier" uses spring vegetables and "aux potates" only uses potatoes.

• Use 600 g of scrag end of neck of lamb (the technical term is, in fact, "collet" or collar) and 600 g of shoulder, all cut into pieces of approximately 80 g each. Remove as much fat as possible.

• Brown the meat on all sides in a casserole. Prepare a bouillon in a container with a bouquet garni, 2 cloves of peeled garlic and 500 g of tomatoes cut in pieces. Pour this over the meat so that it is covered with liquid.

• Leave to cook for an hour, with the lid on, skimming off any fat which may rise to the surface.

Preparation and cooking time
A little over 2 hours
Ingredients
600 g of scrag end of neck of lamb,
600 g of shoulder of lamb,
1 bouquet garni, 2 cloves of garlic,
500 g of tomatoes,
some bouillon, 200 g of turnips,
the same of carrots and potatoes,
300 g of shelled peas

Lamb stew

• Add carrots (200 g), turnips (200 g) and potatoes (same quantity), all cut into pieces. Cook for 30 minutes. The shelled petits pois (fresh) are cooked separately in water for 10 minutes and then added to the dish.

LEG OF LAMB "À LA NINON", "SEVEN O'CLOCK" OR "FROM THE SPOON"

• These different titles do, in fact, describe the same dish which consists of a leg of mutton which has been cooked for such a long time that it can be eaten with a spoon.

• Take a 2.5 kg leg of lamb and remove as much fat as possible. Place it in a high-sided dish on top of 2 carrots cut into thin strips, some thyme, some sage and some bay. Pour a mixture of 5 or 6 spoonfuls of olive oil and a half bottle of dry white wine over the meat. Leave to soak for about 12 hours, turning several times.

• Place the leg of lamb in a stew pot. Seal it in a little hot oil (in order to provoke a rapid coagulation). Pour the marinade and its constituents over the top along with twenty or so cloves of garlic "in their jackets". Fill with bouillon to half way up the leg of mutton. Put

Preparation and cooking time
6 AND A HALF HOURS (NOT COUNTING THE SOAKING TIME: ABOUT 12 HOURS)
Ingredients
1 LEG OF LAMB WEIGHING ABOUT 2.5 KG,
2 CARROTS, THYME, SAGE,
BAY, OLIVE OIL,
1 HALF-BOTTLE OF DRY WHITE WINE,
20 CLOVES OF GARLIC, STOCK

in the oven with the lid on, at a low light, for 6 hours. During the cooking time check that the liquid still reaches to half way up the meat, pour in more if necessary. During the last half hour, remove the lid of the stew pot (whilst still in the oven) so that the liquid can reduce.

• Place on the serving dish with a little of the liquid (put the rest in a sauce boat) being careful not to separate the flesh from the bone prior to serving.

LAMB CUTLETS CHAMPVALLON

• Use 2 cutlets, taken from the best end of neck, per person (a lamb has 10 rib chops which arc callcd cutlets, and 16 loin chops - 6 primary and 10 secondary - the rib chops, or cutlets, are the least fatty although they are interspersed with pieces of fat). Remove as much fat as possible.

• Brown the slices of smoked bacon in some duck fat. The number of slices of smoked bacon should be double the number of cutlets. Put the slices of bacon to one side and seal the cutlets on both sides in the same frying pan.

• Place two layers of potatoes, then the slices of bacon, then the cutlets, then the slices of tomato and rounds of onion, finishing with two or three layers of potatoes cut into medium sized rounds, in a fairly high-sided ovenproof dish. Sprinkle the top layer of potatoes with chopped garlic, thyme and bay leaves. Cover the whole lot with bouillon. Leave to cook on a low light for 1 hour: the bouillon should be entirely absorbed (the success of the dish hangs on this point) and the top should be lightly browned. It is, therefore, important to watch over the cooking carefully, adding extra bouillon if necessary.

Preparation and cooking time
ABOUT 2 HOURS
Ingredients for 4 people:
8 LAMB CUTLETS TAKEN FROM
THE BEST END OF NECK,
16 THIN SLICES OF SMOKED BACON,
8 LARGE POTATOES,
4 TOMATOES,
4 CLOVES OF GARLIC,
THYME, BAY, BOUILLON

GAME

CASSEROLE OF WILD DUCK

• Use a wild duck which has been tamed, leaving the giblets inside (most importantly the liver). Brown, if possible with duck fat (not wild!) in a small stew pot with a lid, over a low light, for 30 minutes.

• Meanwhile, cook 3 carrots cut into small sticks, 4 shallots, 2 onions, 3 cloves of garlic "in their jackets", in a saucepan, without letting them turn golden (i.e. just for a few minutes). Add a tin of concentrated tomato purée, 2 tablespoons of veal glace, thyme, bay, a large glass of white wine and some bouillon (around half a litre, more if the stew pot is quite large). Leave to simmer for 30 minutes on a low light.

• Cut up the duck as follows: remove all the skin (which can be thrown away), put the fillets and thighs to one side (to be kept), take off the wings, break open the carcass and retrieve the giblets which are inside.

Preparation and cooking time
1 HOUR AND A QUARTER, NOT COUNTING
THE TIME SPENT CUTTING UP
AND CLEANING THE WINGS AND THE CARCASS
(WHICH TAKES ABOUT HALF AN HOUR)
Ingredients for 4 people:
1 WILD DUCK,
3 CARROTS, 4 SHALLOTS, 2 ONIONS,
3 CLOVES OF GARLIC,
1 TIN OF CONCENTRATED TOMATO PURÉE,
2 TABLESPOONS OF VEAL GLACE,
1 LARGE GLASS OF WHITE WINE,
50 CL OF BOUILLON, THYME, BAY

• Put the wings, the pieces of carcass and all the scraps of meat left, back in the stew pot. Pour in the sauce from the saucepan. Put the lid back on and simmer for 1 hour.

• Take the pieces of meat out from the stew pot. Remove the wings and the carcass, all of which is edible. Remove the solid ingredients such as the thyme and the bay.

• Put all the scraps and pieces of meat which have been kept at one side back into the stew pot. Heat and serve.

PHEASANT WITH CABBAGE

• This dish can also be prepared with a partridge or a grouse, since pheasants have less and less flavour these days, as they nearly always come from breeding farms.

• Blanch the leaves of 1 green cabbage. Put the 4 largest leaves to one side. Cook the game for about 15 minutes or until it is golden brown on all sides (if possible, use duck fat).

Preparation and cooking time
1 HOUR AND A HALF (NOT COUNTING THE TIME TAKEN FOR SOAKING THE SAUSAGES TO REMOVE THE SALT)
Ingredients for 2 people:
1 PARTRIDGE OR 1 GROUSE,
1 GREEN CABBAGE,
SOME DUCK FAT,
2 SMOKED SAUSAGES,
1 SMOKED SHOULDER OF PORK,
3 OR 4 LARGE CARROTS, SOME BOUILLON,
1 GLASS OF DRY WHITE WINE,
5 OR 6 POTATOES

Pheasant with cabbage

• Remove the salt from 2 smoked sausages (Morteau, Montbéliard) and 1 shoulder of smoked pork cut into two (widthwise).

• Line the bottom of a high-sided saucepan with pieces of cabbage and some carrots. Wrap up the game in the 4 large cabbage leaves, inside of which have been slipped 4 thin slices of smoked bacon. Put it in the saucepan, surrounding it with the 2 sausages and the 2 pieces of shoulder. Cover with pieces of cabbage and with 3 or 4 carrots cut into thick rounds. Add some bouillon and a glass of dry white wine, filling just under half of the saucepan. Cook on a low light for an hour or so. Add the potatoes half way through the cooking time.

HARE STEW

• This recipe takes a long time to prepare but the result is worth the effort!

• You must use a large high-sided stew pot.

• Brown the whole hare (without the offal which will be used later on) over a low light, without a lid on, if possible, in duck fat. Cut 5 large carrots into small cubes along with 4 peeled apples (if possible, an acidic variety), 300 g of button mushrooms and 5 shallots. Pour all this produce into the stew pot, around the hare, with some thyme, a little sage and a dozen or so coarsely ground peppercorns.

• Stir the contents that they do not stick to the pot and pour in 1 litre of crème fraîche and 1 litre of cider. Bring to the boil. **Caution:** be careful not to let it boil over! Cease boiling by removing from the heat.

• Place the stew pot, with its lid on, in a medium oven (gas mark 5 - 6) for 1 hour (this dish must simmer in such a way that the surface is just "quivering").

• Chop up the heart, the kidneys and the liver.

• Take out the pieces of hare and separate the meat from the bones. Remove the solid ingredients and sort them out: all the hard ingredients can be thrown away; the friable ingredients go in the mixer and can then be mixed with part of the cooking liquid in order to obtain a rather thick purée. Now is the time to liberally season the purée with pepper. Put the flesh from the hare back in the casserole along with the purée and heat, adding a little of the cooking liquid.

• It should be noted that if there are any leftovers from this dish, it is always possible to eat them up cold.

BRAISED WILD RABBIT

• This dish can be prepared equally as well with a hare as a rabbit. The main thing is to cook the game in a hermetically sealed receptacle.

Preparation and cooking time
A LONG TIME: DEPENDING ON
THE DEXTERITY OF THE COOK
Ingredients
1 HARE, 5 LARGE CARROTS,
4 APPLES,
300 G OF BUTTON MUSHROOMS,
5 SHALLOTS,
SOME THYME, SOME SAGE,
COARSELY GROUND PEPPERCORNS,
1 LITRE OF CIDER,
1 K̶G̶ OF CRÈME FRAÎCHE
LITRE

Preparation and cooking time
3 AND A HALF HOURS
(+ TIME FOR MARINADING)
Ingredients
1 WILD RABBIT,
100 G OF SMOKED BACON,
1 ONION, 2 TOMATOES,
1 WHOLE GARLIC, 2 GLASSES OF PORT,
400 G OF FRESH SAUSAGES,
10 POTATOES,
400 G OF MUSHROOMS

• Marinade the meat (see page...), which has been cut up into pieces, for several hours. Carefully dry the meat once it has been taken out of the marinade.

• Brown in a cast iron casserole, 100 g of the fatty part of some smoked bacon. Add the meat which must also be golden brown in all its seams. Add 1 onion cut into strips and 2 tomatoes which have been deseeded, peeled and chopped, 1 whole garlic (about 10 cloves) "in their jackets". Moisten with 2 glasses of port. Cook over a low light for 2 hours with the lid on. **Caution:** to prevent the meat from drying up, use a lid with slits in it so that you can add extra water to replace the liquid that has evaporated. After 2 hours add 400 g of fresh sausages, 10 potatoes cut into fairly thick slices and 400 g of mushrooms. Put back on a low light, with the lid on, for 1 hour.

WILD RABBIT WITH TWO SWEET PEPPERS

Preparation and cooking time
45 MINUTES
Ingredients
1 WILD RABBIT,
SOME BOUILLON, SOME VEAL STOCK,
500 G OF GREEN PEPPERS
AND THE SAME OF RED

• Cook a wild rabbit, cut into small pieces, in a casserole until golden brown. In another pan cook 500 g of green peppers and the same of red, cut into thin strips, in some bouillon and a ladle full of veal stock until they are reduced to a pulp. After cooking for 15 minutes over a low light with the lid on, reduce the sauce, at end of the cooking time, by removing the lid. Season, just before placing the whole lot on a serving dish.

Partridge stew

PARTRIDGE STEW

• Brown a young partridge in a stew pot with a little oil and butter mixed together. Once it is golden brown all over, the partridge should be covered with onion compote (see page...), a bouquet garni and several cloves of unpeeled garlic.

• Continue to cook over a low light with the lid on. After 15 minutes add a glass of dry white wine. Continue to cook until the partridge flesh is very tender and has almost come away from the bone.

Preparation and cooking time
45 MINUTES
Ingredients
1 YOUNG PARTRIDGE,
3 LAYERS OF ONION COMPOTE
(SEE THIS RECIPE PAGE...),
1 GLASS OF WHITE WINE, 1 BOUQUET GARNI,
5 OR 6 CLOVES OF GARLIC,
1 TABLESPOON OF OIL AND THE SAME OF BUTTER

JUGGED HARE

• The preparation of jugged hare presupposes a marinade but opinions differ as to the duration of the marinade, from anywhere between 6 and 24 hours. In our opinion, marinading for any longer than 12 hours adds nothing further to the dish.

• Lightly brush a hare, cut up into pieces (preferably small pieces, e.g. one thigh cut into two, one saddle of hare cut into 4 (**why?** because this will make cooking easier and the pieces will have soaked up more of the marinade), with oil.

• The marinade (see page 11) must be made from a strong red wine. Mix well with the hare at least once during the marinade.

• Drain carefully and put all the juice from the marinade to one side, including the liquid drained from the meat.

• Brown the hare in duck fat. Put the meat to one side and throw away the fat. Brown the solid ingredients of the marinade and cook, with the lid on, over a medium light for 1 hour. Check that the meat is thoroughly cooked using the tip of a knife (the flesh must come away from the bone easily).

• Take one ladleful of liquid out of the pan (which remains on a low light) and pour it into a bowl. Gradually add the hare's blood (you can use pig's blood). Mix together thoroughly and pour the whole lot back into the cooking pot.

• Meanwhile, brown the button mushrooms, cut into strips, and some small onions which have, preferably, already been blanched, very quickly in a frying pan. Add these two ingredients on top of the jugged hare which is served on a serving dish (another version adds the mushrooms and blanched onions to the stew 15 to 20 minutes before serving, prior to the end of the cooking time).

Preparation and cooking time
2 HOURS (+ THE MARINADING TIME)
Ingredients
1 HARE WITH ITS BLOOD,
1 MARINADE,
SOME DUCK FAT,
200 G OF BUTTON MUSHROOMS,
200 G OF SMALL WHITE ONIONS,
150 G OF SMOKED BACON

HAUNCH OF VENISON

• There are two ways of thinking, apropos of the preparation of venison (stag or doe). Some (the author being one of these), feel that there is no need to marinade this meat,

Haunch of venison

Ingredients

1 HAUNCH OF VENISON,
1 MARINADE,
4 TABLESPOONS OF OIL,
1 HALF LADLEFUL OF VEAL STOCK,
1 TABLESPOON OF CRÈME FRAÎCHE

that it is enough to leave it to become tender by being left for several hours, covered in oil and seasoning herbs, and then to proceed as if for a leg of lamb, but cooking for a bit longer so that the inside is not too bloody.

• Others like to cover the meat in a marinade for 12 to 24 hours. This marinade is simple: 1 bottle of red wine with onions, 2 carrots cut into rounds, some bay and some peppercorns. Turn the haunch over at least once during the marinading time.

•Take it out, dry it and place it in an ovenproof dish with a little oil. The total cooking time is about 15 minutes per pound.

• Meanwhile, prepare a sauce starting with 2 or 3 ladlefuls of the marinade (from which all of the solid ingredients have been removed). Reduce whilst adding half a ladleful of veal stock. Add 1 tablespoon of crème fraîche.

•Remove the haunch from the dish and carve. Pour the sauce into the dish to mix with the meat juice.

RABBIT

Rabbit with mustard

• Use a rabbit which has been cut up into small pieces. Do not use the liver and the heart (which do not lend themselves to this dish).

• Cover each piece of meat with strong mustard. Arrange these pieces on a dish and put them to one side for several hours.

• Brown the pieces of rabbit and the small peeled onions for 10 minutes in a frying pan, which has been greased beforehand. When the meat is golden brown, take it out of the frying pan and put it into a casserole pot, the bottom of which has been lined with thin slices of smoked bacon.

• Wash out the meat juices from the frying pan with dry white wine and then pour into the casserole. Add some onions and crumble a sprig of thyme and a crushed bay leaf over the top. Put the lid on and leave to cook for 45 minutes over a low light.

Preparation and cooking time
1 HOUR (NOT COUNTING THE TIME
LEFT STANDING COATED IN MUSTARD)
Ingredients
1 RABBIT, 1 POT OF STRONG MUSTARD,
SOME DUCK FAT,
200 G OF SMALL WHITE ONIONS,
200 G OF SMOKED BACON,
1 GLASS OF DRY WHITE WINE,
SOME THYME, SOME BAY,
3 TABLESPOONS OF CRÈME FRAÎCHE

Rabbit with mustard

• When ready to serve, take the pieces of rabbit out of the casserole, thicken the sauce with the crème fraîche and pour into the hot serving dish.

SAUTED RABBIT CHASSEUR

Preparation and cooking time
ABOUT 1 HOUR
Ingredients
1 RABBIT, 2 TABLESPOONS OF OLIVE OIL,
3 TABLESPOONS OF BUTTER,
250 G OF BUTTON MUSHROOMS,
3 OR 4 SHALLOTS, PARSLEY,
1 GLASS OF DRY WHITE WINE,
2 TABLESPOONS OF CONCENTRATED TOMATO PURÉE,
1 TABLESPOON OF MEAT STOCK,
1 SMALL GLASS OF COGNAC

• The expression "chasseur" can be applied to several different types of dish e.g. veal chops chasseur and chicken chasseur, but the preparation is different. For rabbit chasseur, the rabbit should be cut into small pieces (e.g. the thigh into two, the saddle into 3).

• Brown these pieces over a high flame in some oil (2 tablespoons) and some butter (3 tablespoons). Put the lid on and leave to cook over a low light for 30 minutes. Put the rabbit to one side but keep it warm (e.g. in a soup bowl covered with a plate).

• Thinly slice 250 g of button mushrooms. Coarsely chop the shallots (3 or 4) and cut up a small bunch of parsley with scissors. Cook the mushrooms in the cooking dish (only add butter if necessary) for several minutes. Add the shallots and a glass of dry white wine. Bring to the boil and then lower the heat. Add 2 tablespoons of concentrated tomato

Sauted rabbit chasseur

purée and 1 tablespoon of veal stock as well as a small glass of alcohol (marc or cognac). Mix well and put the pieces of rabbit back into the sauce. Serve sprinkled with parsley which has been cut up with scissors.

RABBIT WITH THYME

• Cut a rabbit up into a dozen or so pieces.

• Leave these pieces to marinade in oil in a soup bowl for 15 minutes.

• Place a small sprig of thyme on each piece of meat and roll the whole thing up in a thin slice of smoked bacon.

• Put all this into the dish and cover generously with dry white wine. Cook in the oven on a medium heat for nearly 2 hours. Do not let the meat dry out, there should be plenty of juice left at the end of the cooking time.

Preparation and cooking time
IN TOTAL, ABOUT 2 AND A HALF HOURS
Ingredients
1 RABBIT,
3 TABLESPOONS OF OIL, SOME THYME,
12 THIN SLICES OF SMOKED BACON,
2 GLASSES OF DRY WHITE WINE

RABBIT WITH LEMON

• Brown about 12 small onions, which have already been blanched, and some small pieces of bacon (125 g of smoked bacon), in some butter. Take the whole lot out of the cooking pot and use the fat which has been released to brown the pieces of rabbit (preferably small pieces).

• Put the onions and the pieces of bacon back into the cooking pot. Put the lid on and leave to cook for 45 minutes. After 30 minutes add the crème fraîche and at the end of the cooking time add the juice of one lemon and another lemon cut into rounds. **Caution:** as we know that lemons are now treated with chemicals, it is wise to put the lemon under warm running water whilst it is being cut and rub the skin well.

• Leave to simmer for another 15 minutes to reduce the sauce.

Preparation and cooking time
ABOUT 1 HOUR AND A HALF
Ingredients
1 RABBIT, 12 SMALL WHITE ONIONS,
125 G OF SMOKED BACON,
SOME OLIVE OIL OR DUCK FAT,
PARSLEY, THYME, BAY, SOME BOUILLON,
150 G OF CRÈME FRAÎCHE,
2 LEMONS

RABBIT WITH LENTIL PURÉE

• This is a recipe which was used as far back as the XVIII th century.

• Brown 150 g of smoked bacon, cut into strips, 2 large thinly sliced onions and 1 rabbit cut into pieces, in a casserole with some oil. Cover with bouillon (1 litre) and 2 tablespoons of veal stock. Add some thyme and sage. Leave to cook for 45 minutes over a low heat, without a lid, to reduce the liquid.

• At the end of the cooking time, remove the rabbit and keep covered. Add the purée of 500 g of lentils (see page ...) to the juice which is still warming on the oven, and continue to reduce until you get a thick and unctuous sauce. Put the meat back into the casserole pot for several minutes to warm.

Preparation and cooking time
ABOUT AN HOUR AND A QUARTER
Ingredients
1 RABBIT, 150 G OF SMOKED BACON,
2 LARGE ONIONS, 1 LITRE OF BOUILLON,
2 TABLESPOONS OF VEAL STOCK,
THYME, SAGE, 500 G OF LENTIL PURÉE
(SEE RECIPE ON PAGE 13)

POULTRY

Duck with cucumber

Preparation and cooking time
ABOUT 1 HOUR AND A HALF
Ingredients
1 DUCK, 1 TABLESPOON OF OIL,
500 G OF CUCUMBERS,
1 GLASS OF WHITE WINE,
1 TABLESPOON OF WHISKY

• Peel some cucumbers (500 g in all) and cut them into thick rounds (5 cm). Blanch them for 10 minutes in boiling water. Drain and put to one side.

• Brown a duck with a little oil (hardly any, since the duck is a fatty bird) for 30 minutes first over a high flame and then over a low one in a casserole with a lid on. Then add the cucumbers and the blanched onions. Continue cooking for 30 minutes.

• Take out the duck and leave the cucumbers in. Add a glass of white wine and 1 tablespoon of whisky. Place the cucumbers in the dish with the carved duck and pour the sauce into a sauce boat.

Chicken in a shell of salt

Preparation and cooking time
ABOUT 2 HOURS
Ingredients
1 HIGH QUALITY CHICKEN,
1 KG OF COARSE SALT,
1 KG OF FLOUR,
3 CHICKEN LIVERS, BAY, TARRAGON

• This recipe has the benefit of preserving all the flavour of the chicken so choose a very good quality chicken.

• First of all prepare the shell: mix 1 kg of coarse salt with about 1 kg of flour and some water in a terrine, until you get a paste which does not stick to your fingers.

• Put 3 chicken livers inside the chicken (why? to make the inside unctuous and to give it flavour) 2 bay leaves and 2 sprigs of tarragon.

• Cover the chicken in the paste so that it is completely hermetically sealed. Place it in a pre-heated oven at 150m. Cook at this temperature for 1 hour 30 minutes.

• **Caution:** when carving, the top of the crust must be cut with a knife with a very strong blade in order to remove the chicken.

Chicken in vinegar

Preparation and cooking time
ABOUT 1 HOUR
Ingredients
1 CHICKEN,
3 TABLESPOONS OF OIL,
10 CLOVES OF GARLIC,
20 CL OF WINE VINEGAR,
1 KG OF TOMATOES,
20 CL OF CREAM

• Cut a chicken into pieces and brown them in some oil. Half way through browning, add 10 cloves of garlic "still in their jackets". When the pieces are golden brown, pour out the cooking oil and replace it with 20 cl of wine vinegar. Cover and leave on a low light for 30 minutes.

• Meanwhile, peel and deseed 1 kg of tomatoes. Reduce them to a purée over a low light. When the chicken has finished cooking take it out of the pan along with the cloves of garlic. Pour the tomato purée and 20 cl of cream into the cooking juice. Boil over a low light whilst stirring with a wooden spoon. Coat the pieces of chicken and the cloves of garlic with the sauce when they are on the serving dish.

PIGEON WITH SHALLOTS AND RED WINE

• The traditional way of preparing pigeon is to serve it with petits pois and strips of bacon, but since, it must be acknowledged that the pigeon is quite a bland food, we suggest another recipe.

• Dice some potatoes. Brown them in a frying pan with some butter, over a low light. Meanwhile, bring a bottle of fairly "full bodied" red wine (e.g. côtes du Rhône) to the boil. Add 1 teaspoon of caster sugar, about 12 peppercorns, 1 sprig of thyme and several bay leaves. Leave to simmer (with the surface "quivering" very slightly). Add about 20 whole peeled shallots. Leave the whole lot to reduce and preserve for nearly 30 minutes.

• Brown the pigeon, in some butter, in a casserole with a lid on it (**caution:** pigeon cooks very quickly but must not be bloody, so be very careful) for about 10 minutes. Add the potatoes without the butter that they were cooked in, the shallots and 20 cl of bouillon made with red wine. Leave for several minutes so that all the ingredients reach the same temperature.

Preparation and cooking time
1 HOUR
Ingredients for 2 people:
1 PIGEON, OR 2 IF THEY ARE SMALL,
250 G OF POTATOES,
3 TABLESPOONS OF BUTTER,
1 BOTTLE OF "FULL BODIED" RED WINE,
1 TEASPOON OF CASTER SUGAR,
SOME PEPPERCORNS, THYME, BAY,
20 SHALLOTS

Pigeon with challots and red wine

OFFAL

This word is used to describe not only the internal organs of the animal but also its head and feet. Not all of these parts of the animal are in current use and the recipes that you will find here use only the kidney, the liver and the sweetbread (or thymus).

CALF'S SWEETBREAD

Preparation and cooking time
30 MINUTES
(+ THE SOAKING TIME
AND COOLING TIME AFTER COOKING)
Ingredients for 4 people:
2 OF THE ROUND PARTS
OF A CALF'S SWEETBREAD,
1 CARROT,
8 TO 10 SMALL WHITE ONIONS,
1 GLASS OF DRY WHITE WINE,
SOME WHITE STOCK,
POSSIBLY SOME CREAM,
SOME BUTTER
(DEPENDING ON
THE FINAL METHOD OF PREPARATION)

• This piece of meat is delicate to work with. It is a gland (thymus) which only exists in young animals (calf, lamb). The main thing is to know how to cook and prepare it. There are many ways of preparing it and we will be describing some of them later on.

• The calf's sweetbread is made up of two elements: the round part (300 g) and the

Calf's sweetbread

bunched part (200 g). It is preferable to use the former for the main dish and the latter as a complementary stuffing, e.g for a vol-au-vent or a terrine.

• Soak the calf's sweetbread (more usual nowadays than lamb's sweetbread) in fresh water for several hours. Renew this water at least twice. Place the sweetbread in a saucepan with some cold water. Bring to the boil and then stop the boiling by pouring in more cold water. Drain and place under a board with a weight on top of it. Leave for several hours.

• This is where the difficulty lies: you have to remove the aponeuroses (i.e. the membranes which envelop it and which have a fibrous and sinewy texture) without breaking up the sweetbread. In order to manage this you must press down with your hand, firstly on the sides, and then in the middle, and pull.

• Braise a carrot cut into pieces and some small blanched onions, in a saucepan. Put in the sweetbread and brown on both sides.

• Rinse out the meat residue, left in the pan, with a little white wine and add some veal stock to half way up the sweetbread. This stock is white (see page...). If you wish, you can subsequently prepare the dish with cream or perhaps with brown stock.

• Leave to cook over a low light, with a lid on, for 15 minutes. Remove the sweetbread and put to one side. Put all the cooking juices through a conical strainer.

• Starting, as it were, with this base, you can seek out different accompaniments, e.g. cut the calf's sweetbread into medium sized pieces and coat them with the sauce, adding some small onions which have already been slightly browned, or else pieces of artichoke heart or round slices of courgette which have been blanched and then lightly browned or else simply (if we may say so) some mushrooms such as cèpes, chanterelles or morels).

CHICKEN LIVERS WITH VEGETABLES

• This recipe was inspired by a Hungarian dish but, nevertheless, is perfectly suited to French tastes.

• Brown 5 large onions cut into rounds (preferably red onions) in some duck fat with a little ketchup until they become translucent. Add 4 large tomatoes cut into pieces, some chopped garlic, some parsley cut up with scissors and some meat stock. Bring to the boil and leave to simmer over a low light for 15 minutes.

• Meanwhile, brown some potatoes cut into rounds in a frying pan, also with some duck fat, until they are golden brown on both sides. Put the potatoes into the vegetable pan, add some bouillon if necessary and continue to cook for another 10 minutes.

• **Caution:** there should not be any bouillon left at the end of the cooking time.

• Cook the whole livers over a very high flame in a frying pan and add them to the serving dish with the vegetables. Sprinkle with strong paprika.

Preparation and cooking time
1 HOUR
Ingredients per person:
4 CHICKEN LIVERS,
5 LARGE ONIONS,
4 LARGE TOMATOES,
3 CLOVES OF GARLIC, PARSLEY,
30 CL OF MEAT STOCK, PARSLEY,
KETCHUP, STRONG PAPRIKA,
DUCK FAT,
500 G OF POTATOES

CALF'S KIDNEYS

Calf's kidneys need to be cooked quickly over a hot flame as they can very quickly become dry and hard or else rubbery if they have been boiled. In its natural state, this piece of meat is surrounded by a big, thick shell of fat. Some people like to prepare it in a stew pot, leaving some of the fat still on the meat, this gives it a remarkable "tenderness" (if cooked like this all the cooking juices should be thrown away as they have a distinctive and very disagreeable taste). In general, however, certainly when the kidneys are purchased from a butcher, or a more specifically a retail tripe butcher, the shell of fat will already have been removed.

At this stage there are two new possibilities with regard to preparation: you can either leave the kidneys whole or cut them into strips or pieces.

Calf's kidneys

WHOLE KIDNEYS

• Heat a little butter in a casserole of an appropriate size for the kidney and place the kidney inside it (without a lid) and leave it to cook for 15 minutes, over quite a high flame, turning frequently (with wooden implements so as not to pierce the meat). Take the meat out of the pan and leave it in a dish, 3/4 covered, for 8 to 10 minutes (**why?** because this is the best way of ensuring an even distribution of heat and juices in the meat and a natural exudation of blood. This is far better than the blood pouring out when the meat is cut with the blade of a knife. This procedure is equally recommended for roast beef or leg of mutton).

• After having removed most of the cooking fat, dilute the meat residue, left in the pan, with dry white wine (10 cl). Reduce and add some crème fraîche (2 tablespoons) as well as some meat extract (1 tablespoon) and the juice exuded from the meat.

• If you cut the kidney in two, lengthwise, you can also grill the kidney on a very hot plate without any fat (**caution:** under no circumstances salt the meat prior to cooking or else the escaped blood will prevent the meat from "sealing". See the notes in the chapter "Beef-grilled meat").

KIDNEYS CUT INTO PIECES

• Here you must make sure that all the fatty ligaments are removed. The cooking method is the same as for the whole kidney but obviously much shorter (5 to 8 minutes in the casserole and then 5 minutes away from the heat). The preparation of the sauce is also the same, with all the variations that you can think up.

KIDNEYS CUT INTO STRIPS

• This is the same as above but with an even shorter cooking time. Here, it is, above all, boiling which must be avoided, as boiling has a very undesirable effect on the consistency of the meat.

LAMB'S KIDNEYS

• Each kidney should be cut in two but without separating the two halves and without removing the layer of fat and the sinewy threads. Preparation is similar to that for calf's kidneys but grilling (for brochettes) is the most common cooking method.

• The recipe for lamb's kidneys with mustard should, however, be noted. Open up the kidneys, spread them with a little mustard thinned down with olive oil. Sprinkle with crushed thyme and tarragon. Dip them in a whole beaten egg. Cook the kidneys under a very hot grill, very quickly.

Preparation and cooking time
30 MINUTES
Ingredients for 4 people:
1 CALF'S KIDNEY, SOME BUTTER,
10 CL OF DRY WHITE WINE,
2 TABLESPOONS OF CRÈME FRAÎCHE,
1 TABLESPOON OF MEAT EXTRACT

Preparation and cooking time
10 MINUTES
(COUNTING PREPARATION TIME PRIOR TO COOKING)
Ingredients
2 KIDNEYS PER PERSON

FISH

Recent developments, with regard to methods of transport and refrigeration equipment, mean that we can now use fresh fish in cooking very easily. You should, however, check that the gills are red, the eyes bright and bulging, the body firm and the scales shining.

On the other hand, the fact that fish is more and more frequently being frozen whilst still at sea, immediately after it has been caught, means that the use of frozen fish is highly recommended, certainly when using medium or large sized pieces of fish. Frozen gutted fish, which is often found in the form of fillets, obviously makes for easy use. The question of cooking is paramount. For meat and vegetables, the time lag between being cooked and overcooked is quite wide, but for fish it is very slim and so you must be very careful not to overcook. You should also be aware that it is not as easy to add salt to fish after cooking as it is with meat, as the salt tends to stay on the surface of the flesh. What then are the cooking methods?

The simplest, and thus the most advisable, is oven baking, wrapped in buttered foil (using aluminium foil, closed at the top, so that it may be opened at the end of the cooking time to check on how well done the fish is, and, if necessary, so that cooking may then be finished by exposing the fish directly to the heat). Another method of cooking is "à la meunière" (here the fish is seasoned, lightly covered in flour and cooked in a frying pan with some butter and some oil, being careful not to use too much fat). Fish can also be poached in water, white wine, herbs, onions, shallots etc. It should be noted that there are now various sachets of powder available which can be added to the water and the white wine if you wish to cook the fish in this way.

NORMANDY SOLE FILLETS

Preparation and cooking time
20 MINUTES
(+ TIME SPENT CLEANING THE MUSSELS
AND PREPARATION PRIOR TO COOKING)
Ingredients
8 FILLETS OF SOLE,
1 LITRE OF FARM CULTIVATED MUSSELS,
5 CL OF DRY WHITE WINE,
150 G OF BUTTON MUSHROOMS,
1 TEASPOON OF BUTTER,
1 LEMON,
10 CL OF FISH STOCK,
20 CL OF CREAM,
150 G OF COOKED SHRIMPS

• This recipe takes a long time to prepare and is worth studying carefully.

• Use fillets of sole (1 or 2 per person depending on the size). Cook 1 litre of farm cultivated mussels (after having thoroughly cleaned and scraped them) with a small amount of water and the same of wine (5 cl of each). Cook with a lid on, on a high flame, for several minutes. Take the mussels out of their shells and carefully retain the cooking water and the juice which escapes from the mussels. Leave the mussels in this juice so that they do not dry out as this can happen very quickly. Put to one side.

• Prepare 150 g of button mushrooms, which have been washed quickly under running water and cut into strips, by cooking them for 3 or 4 minutes over a high flame with a little butter, 1 tablespoon of water and the juice of half a lemon. Mix together well during cooking. Cover and put to one side with the cooking juices.

• Place the fillets of sole in a lightly buttered dish and add 10 cl of concentrated fish stock (see page....). Cover with aluminium foil and leave in a medium oven for 10 minutes. Take out of the oven, cover and put to one side (without the aluminium foil), out of the cooking dish where the juices remain. Add to these juices, the cooking juices from the mushrooms and the mussels (as a precaution, strain the mussel juice so that no solids are left in it).

• Mix the three liquids together well, and reduce quickly by heating. Add 20 cl of cream, stirring in such a way as to encourage the liquid to thicken up whilst heating. This assumes that the dish is to be eaten immediately after it has been prepared, if not, the sauce will "turn" because there is no flour in it. Place the mushrooms, the mussels and some cooked shrimps on top of the fillets of sole and coat with the sauce.

Angler Fish cooked like a leg of lamb

ANGLER FISH COOKED LIKE A LEG OF LAMB

• Use a 1 kg piece of angler fish. Insert, as in a leg of lamb, several cloves of peeled garlic, on both sides of the main cartilage. Drizzle with olive oil on both sides, sprinkle with savory and thyme and leave to marinade for 30 minutes.

• Thinly slice 4 onions. Cut 4 small aubergines (leave the skins on), 4 small courgettes and 2 red peppers, into small round discs. Brown the onions in some olive oil in the cooking pot which is to be used for cooking the fish. Add 3 cloves of unpeeled garlic, all the vegetables, as well as 4 peeled and deseeded tomatoes, cut into four. Add some herbs (bay, for example). Simmer over a low light for 30 minutes. Put the fish into the cooking pot with 20 cl of dry white wine. Put in the oven at gas mark 5 and cook for 20 to 25 minutes.

Preparation and cooking time
ABOUT 2 HOURS
(INCLUDING MARINADING TIME)
Ingredients
1 x 1 KG PIECE OF ANGLER FISH,
8 TO 10 CLOVES OF GARLIC,
SAVORY, THYME, BAY,
4 ONIONS, 4 SMALL AUBERGINES,
2 RED PEPPERS, 4 TOMATOES,
20 CL OF DRY WHITE WINE,
5 TO 6 TABLESPOONS OF OIL

CROWN OF ANGLER FISH WITH AIOLI

• Poach 1 kg of angler fish, cut into pieces, in a court-bouillon. Leave to cool and then flake. Beat 8 eggs as for an omelette, add a tin of plain tomatoes and the angler fish. Mix together well until you get an even mixture. Pour the whole lot into a round mould. Cook in a bain-marie for 45 minutes (gas mark 6). Leave to cool and turn out onto a dish garnished with salad leaves. Serve with an aioli sauce.

Preparation and cooking time
1 HOUR AND A HALF
(NOT COUNTING THE COOLING TIME)
Ingredients
1 PIECE OF ANGLER FISH WEIGHING ABOUT 1KG,
8 EGGS, 1 TIN OF TOMATOES,
SOME SALAD LEAVES,
AIOLI SAUCE (SEE RECIPE ON PAGE 18)

COD AU GRATIN

• Soak 600 g of salt cod for at least 12 hours in cold water (skin submerged) to remove the salt, changing the water several times. Peel and chop 4 sweet onions. Leave 3 cloves of garlic in their "jackets". Heat some oil in a casserole pot, add the onions and stir. Add the cloves of garlic. Simmer gently for 10 minutes.

• Meanwhile, peel 4 large tomatoes, deseed them and cut them into slices. Cut 4 sticks of celery into thin strips and cut them into sections. Drain the soaked cod and poach it in water for 10 minutes with the cloves of garlic and the onions, recovered from the other cooking pot. Blanch 200 g of spinach in boiling water and then expel the water by pressing it. Chop coarsely. Spread a layer of onions, which have been reduced to a purée, in the bottom of an earthenware gratin dish. On top of this, arrange, alternating one with another, side by side, the skinned pieces of cod, the slices of tomato, the chopped celery and the spinach with the chopped parsley. Add some chopped garlic. Drizzle with some oil. Put in the oven and leave to cook for 5 minutes on a high heat then sprinkle with parmesan and place under the grill for another 5 minutes.

Preparation and cooking time
ABOUT 1 HOUR
(NOT COUNTING THE SOAKING TIME)
Ingredients
600 G OF SALT COD,
4 ONIONS,
3 CLOVES OF GARLIC,
4 LARGE TOMATOES,
3 STICKS OF CELERY,
200 G OF SPINACH,
OLIVE OIL, PARMESAN

COD BRANDADE

• **Caution:** for all recipes using salt cod follow these instructions carefully. Place the cod in a strainer with feet (e.g a pressure cooker basket) so that it does not touch the bottom of the container. Soak in cold water for 24 hours, renewing the water three or four times.

Cod brandade

Preparation and cooking time
30 MINUTES
(NOT COUNTING SOAKING TIME)
Ingredients
150 TO 200 G OR COD PER PERSON,
8 TABLESPOONS OF OLIVE OIL,
2 CLOVES OF GARLIC,
15 CL OF CRÈME FRAÎCHE,
A FEW CROÛTONS

• In order to poach this soaked cod, place it in a saucepan of cold water. Bring slowly to the boil just until the surface is slightly "quivering". Do not boil (otherwise the cod will go grey). The poaching should last for about 10 minutes. Skim several times.

• Flake the cod. Heat 5 tablespoons of olive oil in a large dish with a thick bottom. When the oil smokes, add the cod and 2 cloves of crushed garlic whilst mixing well with a wooden spoon so as to get a very fine purée, all over a very low light (this is very important). Incorporate 1 or 2 tablespoons of oil, if necessary. Add, whilst still mixing, 15 cl of crème fraîche. Season with pepper and place several croûtons, which have been browned in the frying pan with a little oil, on the serving dish on top of the fish.

HERRING AU GRATIN (FOR 2 PEOPLE)

Preparation and cooking time
ABOUT 30 MINUTES
Ingredients
6 LARGE POTATOES,
8 FRESH HERRING FILLETS,
50 G OF BUTTER,
SOME BREADCRUMBS

• Cut 6 large potatoes into thin round slices.

• Skin 8 fresh herring fillets and remove any bones which may remain. Grease an oven-proof dish with butter and spread a layer of the potato slices on it.

• Arrange the herring fillets on top of the potatoes, one beside the other, then cover with the rest of the potatoes.

• Place 50 g of butter on top in small pieces. Sprinkle with breadcrumbs. Cook in the oven for 25 minutes on a medium heat.

SEA BREAM WITH FENNEL

• Brown 300 g of thinly sliced onions in some olive oil. Add 500 g of raw crushed fennel, 200 g of tomatoes, some thyme and some bay. Cook with a lid on for 20 to 25 minutes with a half-bottle of dry white wine. Oil a gratin dish. Place the sea bream in the dish and cover with the mixture described above. Put the whole lot in the oven for about 25 minutes. This dish may be eaten hot or cold.

Preparation and cooking time
A LITTLE OVER AN HOUR
Ingredients
1 GOOD SIZED SEA BREAM,
300 G OF ONIONS, 500 G OF FENNEL,
200 G OF TOMATOES, THYME, BAY,
OLIVE OIL, 1 HALF-BOTTLE OF DRY WHITE WINE

TUNA AU GRATIN WITH PUMPKIN AND TOMATOES

• Use 1 kg of pumpkin (see the recipe for pumpkin soup) which has been cut into long thick slices. Brush them with oil and place them in a hot oven for about 10 minutes. Then put half into an oiled gratin dish. Mix the contents of a 500 g tin of plain tuna (remove the cartilages and the bones), 300 g of tomatoes which have been peeled, deseeded and reduced to a purée, in oil, in a saucepan, with 3 thinly sliced onions and 2 eggs beaten as for an omelette, together in a large salad bowl.

• Pour this mixture over the slices of pumpkin, cover them with some other slices of pumpkin and with some grated cheese. Put in the oven to cook au gratin (20 minutes on a medium heat).

Preparation and cooking time
ABOUT 45 MINUTES
Ingredients
1 KG OF PUMPKIN,
1 TIN OF PLAIN TUNA (500 G),
300 G OF TOMATOES, 3 ONIONS,
2 EGGS, OLIVE OIL,
150 G OF GRATED CHEESE

BRAISED TUNA

• Soak a thick piece of tuna of about 600 g in weight in some milk for 2 hours. Drain and pat dry. Sprinkle with a very light covering of flour and then brown for 5 to 10 minutes in a shallow frying pan with some olive oil (a large glass). Season with salt and pepper.

• Take out the tuna. Reduce 150 g of onions, 5 or 6 tomatoes, 1 clove of chopped garlic and 150 g of carrots, all of which have been thinly sliced into strips, for 10 to 15 minutes in the shallow frying pan, until they form a pulp (**caution:** do not let them burn).

• Put the tuna back in the frying pan. Add the thyme, the bay and the herbs for seasoning. Dampen with 50 cl of dry white wine and 100 g of crème fraîche. Leave to cook, with a lid on, for 1 hour.

• Serve hot or cold.

Preparation and cooking time
2 HOURS (NOT COUNTING TIME SPENT
SOAKING THE FISH IN MILK)
Ingredients
600 G OF TUNA,
150 G OF ONIONS,
5 OR 6 TOMATOES,
1 CLOVE OF GARLIC, 150 G OF CARROTS,
THYME, BAY, SEASONING HERBS,
50 CL OF DRY WHITE WINE,
100 G OF CRÈME FRAÎCHE,
3 TABLESPOONS OF FLOUR,
1 LARGE GLASS OF OLIVE OIL

HAKE WITH COURGETTES

• Count on one 300 g steak (slice) of hake per person. Leave to marinate for 2 hours after having sprinkled both sides with crushed garlic and fennel, along with some lemon juice. Turn over frequently during the marinading time.

• Blanch some courgettes which have been cut into medium sized round discs, with the skin left on. Place these rounds on the bottom of an oiled dish. Place the hake on top and pour a little tomato purée over the fish. Cook in a medium oven for 30 minutes.

Preparation and cooking time
45 MINUTES
(NOT COUNTING THE MARINADING TIME)
Ingredients
1 x 300 G PIECE OF HAKE PER PERSON,
4 CLOVES OF GARLIC, FENNEL, 1 LEMON,
6 COURGETTES, 1 TIN OF TOMATO PURÉE

BLUE TROUT

• The preparation of this dish is more delicate than is generally believed. The ideal would be to use live trout.

• Stun and kill the trout and then gut it (**caution:** without washing it and taking care not to remove the gluey liquid which covers the skin as it is this gluey film which will turn blue). Place the trout in a dish with the vinegar for several minutes, turn it over so that both sides are thoroughly impregnated (some people advocate boiling prior to soaking in vinegar). Heat the court bouillon and place the trout in it, simmer very, very gently for 10 minutes.

• Serve either with melted butter (caution: not with browned butter), or with lemon.

TROUT WITH RED WINE

• Use a trout of about 250 g in weight, for each person. Gut the fish and leave it whole with the head still on. Wash well as the trout often has a very slimy skin.

• Pour some red Burgundy (one bottle for every 4 trout) into a shallow frying pan. Add 200 g of carrots and the same of onions, all of which have been very thinly sliced, a bouquet garni and 25 cl of water. Bring to the boil, lower the heat and leave to cook for another 20 minutes.

• Pre-heat the oven to 210m. Grease a large dish with butter and arrange the fish head to tail. Fill the dish with court bouillon, prepared as above, to the level of the trout. Leave to cook for 10 minutes, adding more court bouillon if necessary.

Blue trouts

• Meanwhile, reduce 50 to 60 g of very finely chopped shallots to a pulp, in a saucepan, with 20 g of butter. Add the rest of the bouillon which has been passed through a conical strainer. Leave to reduce by a third. Whisk this reduced sauce, adding a little butter if necessary.

• Serve the trout and the sauce separately. Why separately? as the trout still has its bones in it, some people may prefer to remove these bones before the sauce is poured over the fish.

FISH COOKED IN BUTTERED FOIL
(E.G. RED MULLET, SALMON, TROUT...)

• This recipe, which is extremely simple to prepare, can be aided by technological developments, as you will see later when we discuss the use of microwave ovens.

• If a conventional oven is to be used then the fish should, after it has been gutted and wiped, be very lightly oiled and should have some appropriate herbs (e.g. thyme, bay) placed in its stomach. Close the aluminium foil at the top so that it can be opened easily to check on the stages of cooking. The duration of the cooking time and the intensity of the heat vary greatly depending on the size of the fish and the nature of its flesh.

Ingredients

COUNT ON 1 OR 2 RED MULLET
DEPENDING ON SIZE,
1 TROUT PER PERSON,
1 SALMON WILL SUFFICE FOR BETWEEN 4 AND 6
PEOPLE DEPENDING ON ITS WEIGHT,
A LITTLE OIL,
THYME, BAY

Fish cooked in buttered foil

It is impossible to specify an exact time as only direct experience can tell. Do not forget that if you are using defrosted fish, the cooking time will, necessarily, be less than for a fresh fish.

• If you are using a microwave oven, the method of preparation is the same (obviously you should replace the aluminium foil with something else, for example, a soup bowl with a top on it).

SALMON IN BLADDER OF PORK

Preparation and cooking time
1 HOUR AND A HALF (NOT COUNTING TIME SPENT
PREPARING THE BLADDER)
Ingredients
1 PORK BLADDER,
1 X 500 G SLICE OF SALMON,
2 COURGETTES,
2 CARROTS,
1 HALF-BOTTLE OF DRY WHITE WINE,
150 G OF CRÈME FRAÎCHE,
PEPPER

• Cooking in a bladder, which is a very watertight material, means that all the flavours are locked in. Use a pork bladder (you can order this from the butcher) which you will buy ready dried. Fill it with water and then change the water twice to take away any odour. You will notice that it has now clearly grown in size.

• Inside the bladder, place a 500 g piece of salmon with some small round slices of courgette and carrot, some dry white wine (enough to fully cover the fish and the vegetables), some pepper and some crème fraîche (150 g), and mix the whole lot together. Put the bladder, which has been securely fastened with string at the top, in a very large saucepan filled with water. Heat, making sure that the lid is on firmly and put a weight on top of it to ensure that it stays in place. Cook for an hour from the moment that the water begins to boil (then lower the heat to stop the pan from overflowing).

• Take out the bladder and place it in a large soup bowl. Make an incision in one side with the point of a knife or cut the end which is tied up with string, with scissors. Empty all the contents into the bowl and throw away the bladder (this can only be used once).

QUENELLES OF PIKE

Preparation and cooking time
ABOUT 30 MINUTES
Ingredients
500 G OF SEA PIKE FLESH,
200 G OF BUTTER,
200 G OF BREADCRUMBS,
5 EGGS, SALT AND PEPPER,
A LITTLE MILK

Quenelles (seasoned balls or rolls) of sea pike are the most enjoyable of all the different types of quenelles. Their preparation takes place in two parts.

• First of all, the quenelle should be cooked (count on two or three per person depending on the appetite of the guests). Pound the flesh from+ the fish, after having removed the bones (sea pike bones are particularly dangerous), add the butter and the breadcrumbs soaked in milk. Mix well so as to obtain a firm, smooth paste. Add 4 eggs, one at a time, and mix the whole lot together again.

• Put to one side. Divide the mixture into small balls the size of the end of your little finger. Season with salt and pepper and, once again, put to one side.

• Place these quenelles in cold salted water. Leave to poach for 10 minutes, simmering very, very gently (not boiling). The quenelles are cooked when they float to the surface, after having become swollen.

• In the next part of the recipe we go on to dress the quenelles. For this use a sauce which can be made with tomatoes, shallots, white wine or cider and crème fraîche. Thicken this sauce with a beaten egg.

• Either place all the quenelles in a gratin dish, or two by two in small individual dishes. Coat with the sauce. Preheat the oven to gas mark 7 and cook for 5 minutes until au gratin.

DACE FILLETS

This freshwater fish, comes, more precisely, from the lakes of Savoy, and can be enjoyed in several ways. Here, we suggest dace fillet in white wine. This recipe can used with a great many fish (avoid fish whose flesh breaks up easily during cooking).

• Thinly slice the onion and the carrots. Place these in an ovenproof dish and arrange the dace fillets on top. Season with pepper and sprinkle with white wine and the juice of half a lemon.

• Place in an oven preheated to gas mark 7. Turn the fillets over after 10 minutes and continue to cook.

• After having taken out the fillets and the slices of carrot and onion, pass the cooking juice through a conical strainer, mix it with the crème fraîche, heat and pour over the fillets.

Preparation and cooking time
40 MINUTES
Ingredients
1 LARGE DACE FILLET PER PERSON
IF THE DISH IS TO BE SERVED AS AN ENTRÉE,
2 IF IT IS TO BE A MAIN MEAL,
1 ONION,
2 MEDIUM SIZED CARROTS,
1 LEMON,
2 GLASSES OF DRY WHITE WINE,
2 TABLESPOONS OF CRÈME FRAÎCHE,
20 G OF BUTTER, PEPPER

Salmon in bladder of pork

VEGETABLES

Cauliflower with eggs

Ratatouille (stewed vegetables)

• The vital element in the preparation of this dish is to remember to take into consideration the different quantities of water contained in the various ingredients (aubergines, courgettes, tomatoes, peppers). Nothing is more disappointing than a ratatouille for which all the ingredients have been cooked together in one job lot.

• Cut the aubergines into rounds, leaving the skin on. Sprinkle them with salt and place them in a soup bowl with a plate on top and a weight on top of that, so that the vegetable discharges the maximum amount of water possible. Leave them like this for 30 minutes.

• Then put them to cook on a low heat in a shallow frying pan with some olive oil (**caution:** the aubergine will, in any case, "drink up" a lot of oil) and some bay. Leave to cook without a lid, until each piece has been reduced by about a half its size.

• As for the courgettes, they will surrender their water during cooking, along with a thinly sliced onion, in just the same way as the aubergines. Half way through the cooking time add green and red peppers cut into strips (without the seeds of course).

• The third separate stage of cooking is that of the tomatoes, which have been peeled, deseeded and cooked along with some thinly sliced onions, some thyme, some crushed garlic and some unpeeled garlic. Again you must wait for the water to evaporate.

• Next and finally, the products of the three separate stages of cooking should be brought together in the same pan. Cook together for at least 15 minutes (this is not absolute, it all depends on the previous cooking times).

Preparation and cooking time
1 HOUR DEPENDING ON THE SKILL OF THE COOK
IN THE PREPARATION OF THE VEGETABLES
AND HIS ABILITY TO COOK
SEVERAL DIFFERENT THINGS AT THE SAME TIME
Ingredients
4 AUBERGINES,
6 COURGETTES,
5 TOMATOES,
2 RED PEPPERS,
2 GREEN PEPPERS,
6 CLOVES OF GARLIC,
4 LARGE ONIONS,
SALT, OLIVE OIL (A LARGE QUANTITY
MAY BE SOAKED UP BY THE VEGETABLES)

Piperade

• In some respects, this is the ratatouille of south west France. Its name is taken from that of the sweet pepper and it is precisely the presence of this ingredient and the type of fat used (goose or duck fat) which makes the piperade different from ratatouille. The quantities given are for 4 people.

• Place 1 kg of green peppers and 2 or 3 strong red peppers in the oven for several minutes so that the skins can be removed easily. Also remove the pith and the seeds and cut the peppers into strips.

• Cook 4 or 5 onions which have been cut into rounds, 3 cloves of garlic cut into pieces, and the red and green peppers, in the goose fat. Add 1 kg of ripe tomatoes which have been deseeded and cut into large pieces. Leave to cook on a low light, with a lid on, until a thick purée is obtained (take the lid off towards the end of the cooking time so that the liquid can reduce if there is too much left).

• Beat 8 eggs and continue as for an omelette and add the purée whilst still mixing vigorously. Add 4 thick slices of ham which have also been cooked in the goose fat, in the frying pan, earlier on.

Preparation and cooking time
45 MINUTES
Ingredients
1 KG OF GREEN PEPPERS,
2 OR 3 RED PEPPERS,
4 OR 5 ONIONS,
3 CLOVES OF GARLIC,
1 KG OF TOMATOES,
8 EGGS,
4 THICK SLICES OF HAM,
GOOSE FAT

Cauliflower with eggs

Preparation and cooking time
1 HOUR (IF YOUR WORK IS WELL ORGANISED
DURING THE COOKING TIME)
Ingredients
6 LARGE POTATOES,
1 CAULIFLOWER,
6 EGGS,
BÉCHAMEL SAUCE (SEE RECIPE ON PAGE 16),
100 G OF GRATED CHEESE

• Cook 6 potatoes in water in their jackets.

• Separate the cauliflower into florets and cook for 15 minutes in boiling water (make sure that they are not overcooked).

• Use 6 hard boiled eggs. Cut the potatoes into medium sized slices and cut the hard boiled eggs into two.

• Prepare a Béchamel sauce and incorporate 100 g of grated cheese into it. Grease a gratin dish with butter and garnish the bottom with the potatoes, on top of which should be arranged the boiled egg halves. Coat these ingredients with half of the sauce, cover the whole lot with the cauliflower florets and then pour the rest of the sauce over the top. Sprinkle with some grated cheese and cook au gratin in a hot oven for 10 minutes.

Carrots in honey and shallots in cider

Preparation and cooking time
ABOUT 45 MINUTES
Ingredients
400 G OF BABY CARROTS,
400 G OF SHALLOTS,
1 GLASS OF CIDER,
1 KNOB OF BUTTER AND
1 LARGE TABLESPOON OF BUTTER,
1 EQUAL QUANTITY OF LIQUID HONEY

**Carrots in honey
and shallots in cider**

• Cut 400 g of shallots into strips (**caution**: use new shallots, not dried ones). Cook in a small saucepan with a glass of cider and a tiny amount of fat (a small knob of butter) in a medium oven, with a lid on, for 30 minutes. Make sure that the pieces of shallot do not turn brown.

• Steam 400 g of whole new baby carrots. Drain and coat the carrots (with a brush) with a sauce made from 1 tablespoon of butter and an equal quantity of liquid honey. Mix these carrots with the shallots and the remaining cider and heat for a few moments over a low light.

• This dish is well suited as an accompaniment to pork and veal.

Artichokes barigoule

• This is a dish from the south of France for which you need to use small artichokes (reckoning on 4 per person). The only difficulty in the preparation (this must not, however, be underestimated) lies in the first operation. The stem of the artichokes must be cut (only leaving about 4 cm remaining), cut the leaves by about 1 cm and take off two layers of leaves from the base of the vegetable. Next peel the artichoke heart and the stem (use a vegetable knife for this). Rub the heart and the stem with half a lemon and place all the artichokes in a pan with some water and half a squeezed lemon (**why?** so that the artichoke does not go black).

• Take each artichoke, carefully take off the leaves and remove the choke. Put back into the container.

• Cut 1 medium sized white onion and 1 carrot into thin round slices. Chop 2 cloves of garlic with some basil and some parsley.

• Brown the carrots and onions in a casserole pot with some olive oil. Arrange the artichokes in the pot with the tail part uppermost. Add some thyme, some bay and 2 cloves of unpeeled garlic. Pour 5 or 6 tablespoons of dry white wine into the pot and fill with water until the artichokes are covered. Cook, with a lid on, for 15 minutes, on a medium heat, then reduce the liquid over a high flame. At the last moment add the chopped garlic, parsley and basil.

Onion compote

• This dish can serve as an accompaniment for many meat dishes.

• Cut 1.5 kg of onions into very thin round slices (if possible use purple onions). Pour these round slices into a high-sided saucepan with a little neutral flavoured oil of your choice (e.g. sunflower oil) and some butter. Simmer, with a lid on, over a low heat for 30 minutes, taking care that the onions do not stick to the pan and do not go brown. Add some more oil if necessary. Then add 10 cl of wine vinegar and continue to simmer for another 30 minutes. Pour the whole lot into a strainer in order to drain off the excess fat and leave to cool.

• When ready to use, reheat with a little crème fraîche and season with pepper.

Preparation and cooking time
1 GOOD HOUR
Ingredients
16 SMALL ARTICHOKES,
1 LEMON, 1 CARROT, 1 ONION,
4 CLOVES OF GARLIC, BASIL,
PARSLEY, THYME, BAY,
4 OR 5 TABLESPOONS OF DRY WHITE WINE

Preparation and cooking time
1 HOUR AND A QUARTER
Ingredients
1.5 KG OF ONIONS,
SUNFLOWER OIL, BUTTER,
10 CL OF WINE VINEGAR,
50 G OF CRÈME FRAÎCHE, PEPPER

BÉCHAMEL SAUCE (SEE RECIPE ON PAGE 16),
1 TABLESPOON OF OIL, 200 G OF GRATED CHEESE,
POSSIBLY SOME POWDERED GINGER

Preparation and cooking time
30 MINUTES
Ingredients
500 G OF BUTTON MUSHROOMS,
SOME BÉCHAMEL SAUCE

• You can add powdered ginger to the middle layer as the flavour of the ginger goes well with that of the cabbage and sharpens the flavour of the sauce which is, inevitably, quite bland.

MUSHROOM PURÉE IN ARTICHOKE BOATS

• This recipe is an opportunity to illustrate how a food, which has been puréed, can have a very different taste from the taste it has when it is cooked whole. "Nouvelle cuisine" very much overused this characteristic, with its French bean and morel mushroom purées etc. Transformation into a purée is only justified if the new flavour obtained is superior to the original. This is the case with the button mushroom, which is a commonplace product, thus making it different from other mushrooms.

• Quickly wash 500 g of button mushrooms (after having removed the gritty parts) by running them under a tap. Place them over a low heat so that the water evaporates. Put them in a mixer and cook again to evaporate the remaining water, stirring incessantly with a wooden spoon.

Aubergine Gratin

• Mix this purée with the Béchamel sauce and pour it over some artichoke hearts (if these are tinned rinse them well beforehand) which have been heated very quickly in a microwave oven so that the whole mixture is at the same temperature.

AUBERGINE GRATIN

• Choose medium sized aubergines (big ones break up too easily during cooking). Cut into fairly thick round slices, keeping the skin on of course. Blanch for about 10 minutes.

• Oil the bottom of a gratin dish. Spread out a layer of aubergines, coat with tomato sauce and grated cheese (parmesan), then cover with a new layer of aubergines, etc. Coat the top layer just with tomato sauce. Place in a medium oven, having covered the dish with aluminium foil, for 20 minutes. Remove the aluminium foil and sprinkle liberally with parmesan and leave to cook au gratin.

Preparation and cooking time
45 MINUTES
Ingredients
6 MEDIUM SIZED AUBERGINES,
A TIN OF TOMATO SAUCE,
200 G OF GRATED PARMESAN

CABBAGE WITH SPICY SAUSAGE

• This recipe was inspired by a Hungarian dish (cabbage à la Kolozsvar - the hungarian name for the town which is now the Romanian town of Cluj) and has been adapted, since the original is a main dish in itself, whereas this is an accompaniment for roast pork or wild boar.
Blanch a white cabbage and then chop it up.

• Cook some spicy sausage (e.g. the spicy chorizo rather than the mild, for you can get both), cut into round slices with lots of chopped onions, in a frying pan, until the onions become translucent (but not golden).

• Place a little duck fat, a layer of cabbage, a layer of onions and sausage, a layer of cabbage etc., ending with the cabbage, in a casserole dish.

• Drizzle the whole lot with crème fraîche (250 g for 6 people).

• Leave to simmer in the oven, with the lid on, for 1 hour and serve in the cooking dish.

Preparation and cooking time
1 HOUR AND A HALF
Ingredients
1 WHITE OR GREEN CABBAGE,
A SPICY CHORIZO,
300 G OF ONIONS,
SOME DUCK FAT,
250 G OF CRÈME FRAÎCHE

HOT CUCUMBER WITH CREAM

• Cut a large peeled cucumber into cubes. Blanch it in boiling water for 5 minutes and then drain.

• Heat 2 tablespoons of sunflower oil in a frying pan and brown the pieces of cucumber over a medium heat, sprinkled with seasoning herbs, until the water from the vegetable has completely evaporated. Add some cream (2 tablespoons), some lemon juice (1 tablespoon), some nutmeg and some pepper

• Blend carefully. Leave to reduce for a moment or two.

Preparation and cooking time
20 MINUTES
Ingredients
1 LARGE CUCUMBER,
2 TABLESPOONS OF SUNFLOWER OIL,
SEASONING HERBS,
2 TABLESPOONS OF CREAM,
1 LEMON, NUTMEG, PEPPER

POTATOES A LA LYONNAISE

Preparation and cooking time
20 TO 30 MINUTES
Ingredients
6 TO 8 LARGE POTATOES,
SOME BUTTER,
300 G OF ONIONS

• Different varieties of potato are not all used for the same purpose and do not all have the same flavour. Whereas the Bintje is perfectly suited for soups and purées, it is preferable to use Rosa and Roseval for steamed or sautéd potatoes. The queen of the potato is the "Belle de Fontenay" (from which the BF 15 is derived), which is perfectly suited for lengthy cooking (gratins, Champvallon lamb cutlets etc.) as it has a pale grain and always stays firm.

• A recipe for potatoes au gratin is given in the chapter "Mythical dishes". Here we will limit ourselves to describing a recipe for potatoes à la Lyonnaise. This dish not only serves as an accompaniment for numerous meat dishes but is also, in a way, the

foundation of "gigot à la boulangère" (leg of lamb cooked in the oven on a bed of potatoes) in which the potatoes, onions and lamb all cook at the same time. The real recipe for potatoes à la Lyonnaise involves cooking the potatoes and onions separately.

• Cut the potatoes into thin slices. Carefully wash and then dry them. Sauté them in a frying pan with some butter, turning them until they are golden brown on both sides.

• In another frying pan, brown the onions, which have also been cut into thin slices, in some butter, until they are golden brown.

• Add to the potatoes, inserting them in between the layers of potato (the quantity of onions depends on individual taste, but there must always be a lot). Leave them to cook for a few minutes longer.

LEEK PUREE

• Cut 400 g of peeled potatoes into large pieces. Boil them in water for about 20 minutes and then put them into a vegetable press in order to obtain a purée. Put to one side.

•Cook 150 g to 200 g of the white part of the leek, cut into rounds, with butter until they are soft (10 to 15 minutes). Drain.

• Mix the round pieces of leek with the potatoes and 20 cl of crème fraîche. Reheat either in a microwave or in a bain-marie. Seasoning can be with either pepper or nutmeg (this flavouring goes well with leek).

Preparation and cooking time
50 MINUTES
Ingredients
400 G OF POTATOES,
150 TO 200 G OF THE WHITE PART OF THE LEEK,
2 TABLESPOONS OF BUTTER,
20 CL OF CRÈME FRAÎCHE,
PEPPER, NUTMEG

CAILLETTES

• This dish which has a deeply rural origin, is found as much in France (e.g in the Vivarais or in Savoy), as it is in Switzerland (Canton of Grisons). It is based on the use of a much underrated vegetable -' white beet' or 'spinach beet' with its two different elements (the white of the spines and the green of the foliage).

• Blanch 250 g of spinach beet leaf stalks and the same of leaves (prepare separately as the pre-cooking of the leaf stalks is obviously going to be longer than that of the leaves). Drain the leaves thoroughly by squeezing them in your hands. Chop the green part.

• In addition, chop 250 g of pork and 250 g of pork liver. Brown 1 finely chopped onion in some lard, add the meat and then the herbs and season with pepper and garlic.

• Then make balls as large as small oranges out of the mixture, wrap them in caul, squeeze them together in an earthenware dish and cook them in the oven on a low light.

Preparation and cooking time
OVER AN HOUR
(THIS DEPENDS ON HOW THE AGILITY
OF THE PERSON PREPARING THE VEGETABLE)
Ingredients
250 G OF SPINACH BEET LEAF STALKS,
THE SAME QUANTITY
OF PORK AND PORK LIVER,
1 ONION, PEPPER, GARLIC, CAUL

STUFFED VEGETABLES

Three vegetables, in particular, lend themselves to being served with a stuffing: the tomato, the courgette and the aubergine. Of course, all sorts of variations are possible, according to the composition of the stuffing chosen. Here we give three serving suggestions.

STUFFED TOMATOES

Preparation and cooking time
45 MINUTES MAXIMUM
Ingredients per person:
2 LARGE TOMATOES,
150 G OF MEAT FOR STUFFING TOMATOES,
GARLIC, PARSLEY, PEPPER, OIL

• **Caution:** take heed of the following observations:

• In order to remove the maximum amount of liquid from the inside of a tomato which you subsequently wish to stuff, first remove the top and take out the flesh. Place a few grains of rice and some salt inside the tomato and leave in a hot oven for several minutes.

• In order to remove the skin of a tomato (provided that it is not a very hard variety with hardly any flesh inside, as with plum tomatoes), run it quickly under a hot tap and using a very small pointed knife, you can easily peel the skin which is to be removed.

Stuffed aubergines

• It is easiest just to buy the sausage meat that you need for stuffed tomatoes from a butcher as long as you heighten its flavour by adding some parsley, some chopped garlic and some pepper.

• Lightly oil an ovenproof dish (which must have sides as high as the tomatoes themselves) and place the stuffed tomatoes in it and leave to cook on a low light for 30 minutes (watch closely as the tomato's resistance to fire varies greatly depending on the variety). Baste, from time to time, with the juice which is released during cooking.

STUFFED COURGETTES

• Here the stuffing will be made of ready cooked meat.

• Cut the courgettes in two, lengthwise, with the skin still on. Scoop out most of the flesh with a spoon and put it to one side.

• Blanch the courgettes for 4 to 5 minutes in boiling water. Drain.

• Chop 300 g of cooked meat (leftovers from roast pork or veal), 3 or 4 onions, garlic (2 cloves), some parsley and the flesh from the courgettes. Mix and thicken the stuffing with 1 whole egg. Season with pepper, sprinkle with a little grated nutmeg.

• Fill the courgettes with the stuffing and arrange them in a buttered gratin dish. Sprinkle the top with a little grated cheese and put a knob of butter on top of each courgette. Put in a medium oven, lit 20 minutes in advance.

• Leave to cook for about 30 minutes, basting once or twice during cooking.

Preparation and cooking time
ABOUT 45 MINUTES
Ingredients per person:
1 LARGE COURGETTE,
150 G OF COOKED MEAT (PORK OR VEAL),
1 EGG, GARLIC, PARSLEY, PEPPER, NUTMEG,
BUTTER, GRATED CHEESE

STUFFED AUBERGINES

• Here the stuffing is made from vegetables.

• Blanch the whole aubergines for 10 minutes, after having washed and drained them. Plunge them immediately into cold water and leave to relax for 5 minutes. Cut them in two, lengthwise. Scoop out the flesh and put to one side.

• Chop 3 onions and 1 clove of garlic and mix with some peeled and deseeded tomatoes. Reduce the whole lot to a pulp in a saucepan with some parsley and a little powdered cinnamon, in a little oil, for about 20 minutes or until the water from the tomatoes has evaporated.

• Meanwhile, the aubergines, each of which has been drizzled with a teaspoon of olive oil (**caution:** aubergines "drink up" lots of oil) and placed in a gratin dish which has also been oiled, are cooked in the oven (gas mark 6) for 30 minutes (it is wise to cover them with aluminium foil).

• Put the tomato based stuffing in the aubergine halves, sprinkle with lemon juice. This dish can be served hot or cold.

Preparation and cooking time
45 MINUTES PROVIDED THAT THE VARIOUS STAGES
OF PREPARATION ARE WELL ORGANISED
Ingredients per person:
1 LARGE AUBERGINE, 2 ONIONS,
1 CLOVE OF GARLIC, 2 TOMATOES,
PARSLEY, CINNAMON, OIL

CHEESE

According to French tradition, a meal most often includes cheese prior to dessert. There is an abundance of different cheeses to choose from, but the recipes which follow rely on the use of hot cheese and are, therefore, radically different from the usual concept of cheese chosen from a "cheese board".

TOASTED CHEESE SLICES

• Use medium or large slices of stale bread. Moisten with a few drops of white wine and place in a gratin dish with a slice of unfermented boiled cheese (of the type which is commonly called "raclette"), the slice of cheese must be quite thick. Put in a preheated oven (gas mark 7), and leave long enough for the cheese to melt and cook slightly au gratin. Season with pepper according to taste (certainly do not add salt, the cheese itself is already salted and cooking will concentrate the salt content even more).

Preparation and cooking time
15 MINUTES
Ingredients per person:
2 GOOD SIZED SLICES OF BREAD,
A LITTLE WHITE WINE,
2 SLICES OF "RACLETTE" TYPE CHEESE
(OR BEAUFORT, OR COMPTÉ, IN SHORT,
A COOKED CHEESE), PEPPER

CHEESE FONDUE

• This is a complete dish in itself but it must be balanced a little, by having a little smoked ham beforehand and then a salad afterwards.

• This dish originates in the Alps, but only in the French and Swiss slopes, since it is not found in German or Italian cuisine, even though the basic ingredient (a "mountain", full fat, boiled cheese, rich in fat) is produced throughout the Alps. Its success with tourists, there for the winter sports, basically led to certain off-shoots of the original basic recipe, which never used mushrooms or cornflour to make the fondue "take", or crème fraîche or eggs. These additions are no more than heresies provoked by the desire to do something "new" in the fierce competition existing between hotels and restaurants.

• Quantities given here are for 6 people (the fondue is, in general, a dish to share with guests) but let us first of all describe the special apparatus which you will require: a small, fairly high sided, earthenware pot; an alcohol burner, the temperature of which can be regulated; a long handled wooden spatula; special long handled forks with two prongs.

• Amounts to prepare: 600 g of Swiss cheese of the type made in Fribourg (not to be confused with the Franco-Swiss cheese made in the Jura which is a fermented cheese), 300 g of another full fat, boiled cheese, with a stronger flavour (i.e. a more mature "mountain" cheese), a bottle of dry white wine.

• Rub the bottom of the fondue pot with a clove of peeled garlic. Pour in three quarters of the bottle of wine and place the fondue pot on the burner which is turned full on. Wait until a little vapour is released from the white wine and then put in the cheese, cut into small cubes, and begin to stir the mixture continuously, always stirring in the same direction (this helps the cheese to melt).

• Half way through, add a small glass of a white spirit (kirsch, for example). Wait until the mixture becomes extremely unctuous and then lower the heat of the flame. All that remains is to gather around the fondue and to dip in some pieces of bread with the forks described above.

• When nearly all of the fondue has been eaten, increase the heat so as to brown the cheese left at the bottom which is delicious (although clearly more salty than the fondue itself). Scrape it out with the spatula and share it out.

DESSERTS

BITTER CHOCOLATE MOUSSE (FOR SIX PEOPLE)

• Break 200 g of bitter chocolate into small pieces in a bowl. Add 10 cl of very hot, strong coffee and 30 g of cocoa (powdered). Place in a bain marie and mix until melted but without curdling. Put to one side, still in the bain marie.

• Take 12 egg whites and beat them with a whisk in a salad bowl. Gradually incorporate 100 g of caster sugar as soon as the egg whites have formed "peaks". Beat with the whisk to ensure the firmness of the mixture.

• Pour the part of the chocolate which is still warm, into another salad bowl with a quarter of the stiffened egg whites and mix well. Then carefully pour in the rest of the stiffened egg whites, mixing very gently with a wooden spoon. Leave to cool for several hours in the refrigerator.

Preparation and cooking time
30 MINUTES
(NOT COUNTING THE COOLING TIME)
Ingredients for 6 people:
200 G OF DARK CHOCOLATE,
10 CL OF VERY STRONG COFFEE,
30 G OF POWDERED COCOA,
12 EGGS (ONLY THE WHITES),
100 G OF CASTER SUGAR

Bitter chocolate mousse

Apple gateau

APPLE GATEAU

• In a large salad bowl, mix together 1 kg of peeled apples cut into slices, 5 table-spoons of flour, the same quantity of sugar, 2 whole eggs, 100 g of butter, 2 packets of sugar flavoured with vanilla (this is optional), 1 pinch of salt and 1 packet of baking powder.

• Grease a cake tin with butter and place the mixture inside it. Cook in a medium oven for 45 minutes.

CHERRY CLAFOUTIS (FOR 6 PEOPLE)

Preparation and cooking time
45 MINUTES
Ingredients
500 G OF CHERRIES, 3 EGGS, 100 G OF SUGAR,
100 G OF BUTTER, 50 G OF FLOUR

• Wash and remove the stalks from 500 g of cherries. Arrange the cherries next to each other in a clafoutis mould greased with butter. Meanwhile, mix together 2 egg yolks then add 100 g of sugar and blend for a long time. Add 1 whole egg, mix. Add 100 g of creamed butter, 50 g of flour, 50 g of starch. Mix again for a long time. Finally, add 25 cl of milk and a glass of kirsch.

• This mixture must be a very liquid paste. Pour it over the cherries in the mould. Cook for about 30 minutes in a hot oven (180m).

AND THE SAME OF STARCH, 25 CL OF MILK,
1 GLASS OF KIRSCH

FROZEN CHOCOLATE SOUFFLE

• Put 5 egg yolks and 80 g of caster sugar in a saucepan in a bain marie. Whisk until the mixture thickens up. Meanwhile, melt 150 g of chocolate, broken into small pieces, in a small saucepan with a tiny amount of water, over a low light. Add the melted chocolate to the first mixture in small doses, continuing to whisk.

• Beat the 5 egg whites until they are stiff. Add to the mixture along with 100 g of Chantilly cream.

• Line a souffle dish with aluminium foil, open at the top (extending about 5 or 6 cm beyond the top of the mould). Pour the mixture into the dish and place it in the freezer compartment of the refrigerator and leave it there for a few hours. Remove the aluminium foil prior to serving.

Preparation and cooking time
20 MINUTES
(NOT COUNTING THE FREEZING TIME)
Ingredients
5 EGGS, 80 G OF CASTER SUGAR,
150 G OF CHOCOLATE,
100 G OF CHANTILLY CREAM

Cherry clafoutis

CHOCOLATE GATEAU

Preparation and cooking time
A LITTLE OVER AN HOUR
Ingredients
140 G OF CHOCOLATE (DARK CHOCOLATE IF POSSIBLE),
THE SAME OF CASTER SUGAR, 70 G OF BUTTER,
4 EGGS, 90 G OF FLOUR,
1 TEASPOON OF RUM

• Break the chocolate into small pieces and melt it in the butter over a very low light. Add the egg yolks, one after another, and then the flour and the sugar.

• Next pour in the four beaten egg whites and the rum.

• Place the whole lot in a cake tin, which has been well greased with butter, and cook on a low light for 50 minutes.

CHESTNUT LOG

Preparation and cooking time
2 HOURS (NOT COUNTING THE TIME
IN THE REFRIGERATOR: SEVERAL HOURS)
Ingredients
1 KG OF CHESTNUTS,
75 CL OF MILK,
250 G BAR OF CHOCOLATE,
100 G OF BUTTER,
1 TABLESPOON OF SUGAR

• Make incisions in the chestnuts, right around their circumference, cutting through both skins. Blanch them for 2 minutes in boiling water and remove the two skins.

• Bring the milk and sugar to the boil, immerse the chestnuts in the liquid and leave to cook for 30 minutes over a low light. Put the milk and the chestnuts through the Moulinette (vegetable grinder), and add the butter.

• Melt the bar of chocolate in the tablespoon of water in the bain marie. When the chocolate is fully melted mix with the water and then mix again with the chestnut purée.

• Place the whole lot on a sheet of aluminium foil and make a roll. Close the sheet of aluminium foil securely and place in the refrigerator.

UPSIDE DOWN TART OR TARTE TATIN

Preparation and cooking time
45 MINUTES
Ingredients
250 G OF CASTER SUGAR,
125 G OF BUTTER,
2 KG OF APPLES,
PASTRY FOR THE TART

• This dish is a little bit of a legend in that it would have been created by the spinsters Tatin and Sologne. It is a tart made with caramelized apples and short pastry (excellent frozen pastry is now available).

• The main problem lies in the preparation of the sugar. It is advisable to use a Pyrex type dish for this recipe so that you can watch its development. Pour 250 g of caster sugar into the dish so as to get a very even layer. Distribute 125 g of butter, cut into small pieces, over the top of the sugar and gently pour a half glass of water over the top of that.

• Peel 2 kg of apples (with firm flesh and not very acidic). Cut them into two, remove the pips and the cores. Arrange these apple halves over the damp sugar, squeezing them up together, one against the other, standing upright.

• Place the mould over a medium light (**caution:** if you are using a pyrex dish think about using an asbestos plate in order to avoid direct contact with the heat). As soon as the syrup boils, reduce the heat. The cooking time lasts for about 30 minutes.

• What is happening? The water poured over the sugar stops it from burning; the butter melts, mixes with the sugar and so makes a fatty, sugary syrup. The apples will cook but without becoming misshapen. The water evaporates, the butter is absorbed by the apples and a caramel is formed from the sugar.

• The cooking must be considered to be at an end when the syrup at the bottom of the mould turns a light caramel colour.

• Whilst this is cooking, roll the pastry (rolled out on a lightly floured surface) into a round shape, slightly larger than the width of the dish. When the cooking is over, place the pastry over the apples so as to completely cover them, with the pastry crimped at the edges of the dish.

• Place in a hot oven for about 30 minutes. Turn the mould out onto the serving dish. To be eaten hot or warm (**caution:** do not let it cool for too long or else the caramel dampens the pastry)..

Chestnut log

MYTHICAL DISHES

These are dishes, whose recipes are passed down, jealously and almost religiously, from mother to daughter, from father to son, from chef to commis chef. They are also the dishes which enthusiasts discuss with lively comments and exclamations, passing on the names of restaurants (preferably a little "bistro" not yet discovered by the guide books) which, in their opinion, are the best places in which to taste them...

With regard to these dishes, we shall endeavour to respect the principle of regional impartiality by describing regional variations to the ingredients or to the method of preparation, but, inevitably, a choice must be made when it comes to the recipe given as reference, and some people, perhaps justifiably, will judge that we have been biased!

What are these dishes? Cassoulet (ragout of meat and beans), coq au vin, bouillabaisse, blanquette de veau (veal stew), daube (braised beef), potée (ham stew), pot-au-feu (boiled beef with vegetables), gratin de pommes de terre (potatoes au gratin), baekhofen (beef, mutton and por- with vegetables), lièvre à la royale (hare à la royale), chou farci (stuffed cabbage).

On previous pages:

The famous Alsatian sawerkraut and meats.

POTEE (HAM STEW)

This dish has many regional variations, this multiplicity being due to the nature of the ingredients used. The recipe which is given here can, therefore, easily be altered or added to.

• Use 1 kg of slightly salted loin of pork. Soak for several hours in cold water in order to remove the salt. Change the water at least twice.

• Place the loin of pork and a fresh ham joint in a large cooking pot with lots of cold water. Bring gradually to the boil, skimming off all the impurities which rise to the surface. Stop the water boiling by adding a little cold water. Skim again (this time the scum will be white and not dark coloured as before) and leave to cook (bubbling gently) for at least 1 hour. Then, if you wish, add some smoked sausages (**caution**: no Strasbourg sausages or frankfurters as their consistency is not suitable for slow cooking).

• Meanwhile, prepare the vegetables: carrots, turnips, leeks and a cabbage (to be blanched). Place all these vegetables (still whole) in the cooking pot and start to gently simmer again for over 2 hours. Then add some potatoes (a variety which is not liable to break up during cooking) and cook for a further 30 minutes. Sometimes pears and apples are added at the same time as the potatoes.

CASSOULET (RAGOUT OF MEAT AND BEANS)

The cassoulet is prepared lovingly over a period of at least two days and there is a precise order to the procedures that must be followed. We are assuming that this dish is being prepared for a meal for 8 people

• The dish is based on dried "ingot" type haricot beans (1 kg). Soak them in water for 12 hours. Normally, these beans, which start off by floating, will become immersed in the water. Blanch them by bringing the cold water to the boil. Leave to simmer gently for at least 30 minutes. Change the water and repeat the operation (for about 1 hour). Check that the haricot beans are well cooked but make sure that they do not end up as pap. Throw away the water and put the beans to one side.

• While the beans are cooking, place 200 g of fresh bacon rind cut into pieces, a raw pig's trotter or calf's foot, cut in two lengthwise (**why** do we need the foot? To produce the jelly which gives the cassoulet the luxurious texture which is so vital) in a saucepan with an onion and some herbs (tarragon, sage). Bring to the boil and leave to cook for 15 to 30 minutes.

• Remove the pig's trotter, put the pieces of bacon rind to one side and carefully retain the cooking water.

• Cut 400 g of loin of pork (a tender and relatively fatty cut of pork) and 500 g of Toulouse sausages into pieces and brown them in a frying pan with a little goose fat (or at any rate some butter or some oil!), some coarsely chopped onions and some garlic (2 or 3 finely chopped cloves).

• After cooking (for about 10 minutes), put the whole lot to one side in a dish after having poured the cooking juices from the pig's trotter into the frying pan in order to swill out the cooking juices which will then be added to the meat.

• Take a large earthenware dish (without a lid) and place in it, the haricot beans, the meat which has been cooked or rather "sealed" in the frying pan, some pieces of preserved duck or goose (e.g. the wings or neck rather than the thighs which are too fatty) and 3 or 4 tomatoes cut into pieces. Mix well so that the meat is evenly distributed. Pour in the cooking juices from the pig's trotter. This liquid should have completely disappeared by the end of the cooking time.

• Put the whole lot into the oven on a low light for at least 1 hour. When the top is browned, break this crust by turning it over and mixing it in; repeat the procedure. The total cooking time can last as long as 2 hours (this depends on the haricot beans).

• Leave to cool. Reheat in the oven prior to serving in the dish in which it has been cooked.

COQ AU VIN

This esteemed dish can be prepared in a number of different ways (over thirty!) according to the region of origin. The variable ingredients in these recipes are essentially the liquid (red wine, white wine, beer) in which the chicken cooks and the ingredients which surround it (bacon, mushrooms etc.).

Here we will give the "traditional" recipe first and then go on to describe several variations. Firstly, you should realise that we are not talking about a real cock but a chicken and that the choice of a good vintage wine is not really necessary. This is, fundamentally, a simple country dish which should retain its rustic qualities.

• Cut the chicken into pieces (this can be done perfectly well by the butcher from whom you purchase the bird). Obviously, if possible (if you live in the countryside for example) you should obtain a little chicken's blood, but don't be under too many illusions as this traditional ingredient risks the failure of the dish. In order to store this blood, pour some vinegar into the container with it (so as to prevent clotting).

• Take a casserole pot, preferably a cast iron one (as this material encourages the liquid to "simmer"). Brown the pieces of cock/chicken with some oil and some butter. Add some pieces of bacon (one small word of advice: if you blanch these pieces of bacon beforehand they will not dry up during roasting) and some onions.

• When the pieces of meat are browned, add some good quality red wine (e.g. a red burgundy made from mixed Pinot and Gamay grapes), a bouquet garni, some mushrooms (e.g. button mushrooms), according to individual taste, and several unpeeled cloves of garlic. The wine should cover all the ingredients but not drown them.

• Do not, of course, allow to boil and leave to cook for over 1 hour on a low light, depending on the size of the chicken (the flesh should come away from the bone easily). Remove the lid at the end of the cooking time to reduce the sauce if too much remains.

• If you are using chicken's blood, this must be incorporated into the sauce at the end of the cooking time. In order to do so, take a ladleful of the sauce and put it to one side in a small container. Pour it slowly onto the blood, gently stirring the mixture so that the two elements merge together without curdling. Pour the whole lot back into the cooking pot, mix well. Add some croûtons of toasted bread. As an accompaniment, serve potatoes with finely chopped parsley.

• **Some regional variations:** with riesling (riesling wine from Alsace, mushrooms and cream added at the end of the cooking time), à la normande or Vallée d'Auge (cooking in butter, 2 apples cut into small cubes, cider and cream added at the end of the cooking time; no wine or bacon; as an accompaniment, replace the potatoes with apples); à la basquaise (use white wine, tomatoes, garlic, cèpes and oil for cooking).

• Generally speaking, the use of mushrooms (for the "traditional" recipe use button mushrooms) is desirable but is not an absolute rule.

BOUILLABAISSE

In the opinion of the inhabitants of Marseilles and its surrounding area, and also according to its own esteemed reputation, there is only one real bouillabaisse, and that is the one which comes from the Marseilles region itself.

• The vital thing with this dish is to use lots of different sorts of fish: conger eel, John Dory, scorpion fish, grey sea bream, angler, red mullet, whiting etc.

• Scale, gut and clean the fish. Remove the fins and tails (but leave the heads). Cut into medium sized sections and put into two separate lots, on the one hand the "tender" fish like the whiting, the red mullet and the John Dory (as these can be cooked more quickly) and on the other the "firm" fish like the conger eel and the scorpion fish.

• Use a very large "faitout" type stew pan. Brown some onions and some thinly sliced garlic with a little oil, olive oil of course, some peeled and deseeded tomatoes, some sweet pepper cut into strips, some parsley, some thinly sliced fennel, some thyme, some bay (the bouillabaisse must be a celebration of seasoning herbs!). Add 2 litres of water and some coarsely ground pepper and simmer for 10 minutes. Next add the "firm" fish, bring to the boil for 5 minutes, add the "tender" fish and again bring to the boil for 5 minutes. Put the pieces of fish to one side and keep warm. Reduce the stock a little over a low light. Place the fish in a large soup tureen and pour the stock over the top. Add some small croûtons of bread moistened with olive oil.

VEAL STEW

• Be selective when you choose the veal that you are going to use. For 4 people reckon on about 1.5 kg of shoulder (some people use a mixture of shoulder, breast and best end of loin, but shoulder is preferable). Cut up into 60 to 70 g pieces and place in a saucepan with some slightly salted water. Bring to the boil and leave for several minutes, skim, pour in fresh cold water and drain.

• Put the meat back in a saucepan which is just about big enough to contain it. Cover with white stock made with bouquet garni, 2 onions, 1 clove of unpeeled garlic. Put the lid on tightly, bring to the boil and leave to simmer for 40 minutes.

• Braise 200 g of whole white mushrooms and retain the cooking juices. Blanch 200 g of small onions. Put two ladlefuls of juice, which has been put through a conical strainer, into the saucepan in which the meat was cooked. Mix together with the cooking juices from the mushrooms and with 50 g of crème fraîche. Reduce and add 3 or 4 ladlefuls of meat juice which has also been put through a conical strainer.

• Beat the 4 egg yolks with 4 tablespoons of cream. Add a little nutmeg and pour the whole lot, spoonful by spoonful, into the sauce. Add the mushrooms, the onions and the juice of one lemon. Heat but do not allow to boil. Add the pieces of meat. Pour the whole lot into the serving dish and sprinkle with chopped parsley.

DAUBE (BEEF STEW)

It is quite an uncommon occurrence that a dish should give its name to the receptacle in which it is prepared. We should say that the "daubière" or stew pot is longer than it is wide, almost oval in shape, with a lid which fits tightly to the pot itself ensuring sealing tightness during cooking.

Several types of meat can be used to make a stew, duck for example, but the basic ingredient is beef and more precisely the cut which is called the topside (caution: not the silverside which is less tender) situated at the back of the animal just above the shin.

Our recipe uses the cheek of beef which is, in our view, particularly suited to this dish because of its tenderness and its capacity to join with the jelly released by the calf's foot.

• Take a stew pot (**caution:** do not stint on size as the calf's foot has a tendency to rise up during cooking, pushing off the lid and so you must used a pot with as tight a fitting lid as possible).

• Line the base of the stew pot with a calf's foot cut in two, lengthwise. Place 1.5 to 2 kg of cheek of beef, 200 g of unsmoked bacon cut into thin pieces, 4 tomatoes (which have had their skins removed under a hot tap), 1 kg of carrots which have been peeled and cut into thick rounds, 5 or 6 peeled cloves of garlic, 8 or 10 stoned prunes and 2 large handfuls of dried currants, some herbs (fresh if possible), sage, tarragon, basil, (no rosemary as the bits disperse and are unpleasant for guests), in the pot. The whole lot should be covered, if possible, with a full bodied red wine (e.g. côtes-du-rhône). In addition, add the contents of a tin of concentrated tomato purée.

• Place the stew pot, with the lid on, in the oven, on a low light for 3 hours, checking the level of the liquid every hour and filling it back up if necessary. After 3 hours, turn off the oven and leave to cool gradually until the following day.

• The next day, sort out the ingredients in the pot. Remove the sprigs of herb, and the calf's foot. Cut the meat into medium sized cubes and put them back in the pot. Cover again with red wine and put the oven back on at a low light for 2 hours, after having tasted to see whether you need to add salt and pepper. Leave to cool, once again, after cooking.

• The third stage of cooking, which is really a reheating, will take place just before the meal. Serve steamed potatoes or macaroni as an accompaniment.

POT AU FEU (BOILED BEEF WITH VEGETABLES)

This very ancient recipe brings together, in one big cooking pot, various different cuts of beef and some vegetables which are cooked slowly on a low heat so that they cook in a stock which forms during the cooking itself.

• About which, a word of warning: choose your cuts of meat well. Opinions differ as to which cuts should be selected but the main thing is to use ingredients which complement one another. For example, some silverside (rear, exterior cut of meat) which is lean, some chuck steak (from the shoulder) some top ribs (upper part of the ribs) which are appreciably more fatty and some tail (used for the gelatine that it releases). You must also use marrow bones (several).

• A second word of warning: it is useful to decide prior to commencing the preparation whether the main objective is to obtain an excellent stock or whether the pot-au-feu is, in itself, the main preoccupation. The two objectives are, in fact, a paradox. In order to obtain a stock the cuts of meat must be plunged into cold water, whereas with the second objective you must start off with boiling water.

• Once you have decided how to start the dish, the preparation is the same.

• Fill a large cooking pot with cold salted water (1 tablespoon) and put in the pieces of meat. Skim as the cooking progresses. When the pot starts to boil add some vegetables (500 g of leeks, 500 g of whole carrots, 200 g of celery sticks, some onions, a bouquet garni), some salt (if possible, coarse salt), some pepper and a clove. Some people also use turnips.

• Simmering should continue for at least 4 hours. The marrow bones are poached in this stock with the meat and vegetables, several minutes prior to the end of the cooking time.

• The dish is eaten in two stages. The meat and vegetables should be eaten straight away, but it is advisable, to leave the bouillon for a while. First put the hot bouillon through a fine strainer and then leave it to cool. Remove the fat which has deposited itself on the surface and then reheat.

• It should be noted that you can prepare a small "pot-au-feu" containing a knuckle of veal cut into slices. With this dish you need to cover both sides of the marrow bones with salt (**why?** to ensure that the marrow does not escape into the bouillon).

POTATOES AU GRATIN

• **What a lot of epithets have been applied to this dish! Dauphinois, savoyard, campagnard etc. The one which really describes potatoes, simply cooked au gratin, is "savoyard". There are several variations which we will give at the end of the recipe when we shall advise against them.**

Here is our suggested recipe which, in our opinion, has the advantage of referring to its origins which are, in some respects, historic. It is a dish which was prepared by peasants, more precisely by highlanders living with their stock, who merely used the products which they had directly to hand.

• Peel some potatoes which are not likely to break up during cooking. Cut them into very thin round slices, dry them by placing them on a tea towel (this is vital as it enables them subsequently to be impregnated by the cream). Take an earthenware dish (any other material - glass, copper, aluminium - will give a different flavour, try it!). Rub the bottom of the dish with the garlic and arrange two layers of potatoes, then a layer (thin) of grated cheese and 4 tablespoons of cream, then two more layers of potatoes etc., ending with a layer of cream. Put in a hot oven, on a medium heat, for 30 to 45 minutes. Finish the cooking off with 10 to 15 minutes at a high temperature, after having added a final layer of grated cheese to the dish (this is so as to get an "au gratin" effect without the dish drying out.

• If you are not sure of the cooking time, place a piece of aluminium foil on top of the dish at the start of cooking which will allow you to check that the bottom does not stick. The aluminium foil should, of course, be removed prior to the end of the cooking time.

• Ingredients which we feel have no place in this recipe are: bacon, bouillon (!), an egg (!!), nutmeg (!!!). On the other hand, if you want to make the dish more tasty, do not hesitate to sprinkle the layers with tiny pieces of garlic.

BAEKHOFEN (BEEF, MUTTON AND PORK WITH VEGETABLES)

The name of this Alsatian dish comes from the method of cooking: cooked in the baker's oven (it can also be spelt baeckeoffe). It can, however, be prepared perfectly well in a pressure cooker which shortens the cooking time whilst retaining the different flavours, this being the main objective of the preparation.

• For 6 to 8 people, use 500 g of loin of pork, 500 g of shoulder of mutton (with the bone taken out), 500 g of beef chuck steak or neck of beef. To make it easier to serve at the table, it is preferable to cut these pieces of meat into medium sized pieces whilst still raw. On the eve of the preparation, place these pieces of meat in a marinade which should cover them completely: 250 g of chopped onions, the white part of 2 or 3 leeks, half of a celeriac, 1 carrot cut into rounds, thyme, bay and dry white wine.

• On the day that the dish is to be prepared, place a layer of potatoes cut into medium sized rounds, the beef, some slices of potato, the mutton, some slices of potato, the pork and then, finally, some more potatoes cut into rounds, into the pressure cooker. Pour the marinade and the vegetables from the marinade over the top. This should fully cover the meat and potatoes.

• Leave to cook on a low light for 1 hour and 15 minutes from the time when the pressure cooker is closed.

HARE A LA ROYALE

• **This dish can be prepared according to two recipes, one of which smacks of true professionalism whilst the other can be followed by an amateur. We decided, by way of an exception, that it would be beneficial to give both recipes.**

For a professional
• Bone an entire hare, being careful not to tear the stomach flesh too much. Remove the flesh from the paws and chop it with the liver, the heart and the lungs as well as with 200 g of uncooked foie gras and 100 g of fresh bacon.

• Add to this mixture, 100 g of breadcrumbs soaked in stock and pressed, 1 spoonful of chopped onion, cooked in butter until it is reduced to a pulp, and a very tiny crushed tip of garlic, 150 g of chopped truffles and a pinch of parsley. Thicken this stuffing with the hare's blood and season well.

• Fill the hare with this stuffing. Sew up the skin of the stomach so as to thoroughly envelop the stuffing. Braise the hare in red wine court bouillon for about 2 hours, basting it frequently throughout the cooking period. Drain the hare, baste it with its braising stock to which will have been added 1 spoonful of armagnac and some diced truffles.

For an amateur
• This is a recipe which takes a long time to prepare and which should be spread over two days as the dish can be reheated perfectly adequately.

• Use a stew pot with a lid. Grease the bottom and the sides with duck or goose fat and place the hare, which has been gutted and has had its head and tail removed, in the stew pot, lying on its back. Endeavour to make use of the blood which can be preserved with some vinegar.

• Add 1 diced carrot, 4 onions, 20 peeled cloves of garlic, 40 cloves of shallot, also peeled, and a bouquet garni. Pour in large glass of red wine vinegar and a bottle and a half of good non-vintage burgundy. Place the cooking pot, with the lid on, over a low and constant heat for the first stage of cooking which is to last for 3 hours.

• Meanwhile, first chop 125 g of unsmoked bacon, then the heart, the liver and the lungs, then 10 cloves of garlic and 20 cloves of shallot, separately and as finely as possible. Mix them all together so as to get an even mixture.

• When the first stage of cooking is over, proceed as follows:

— remove the hare from the cooking pot and take out the bones which have become detached. Remove the bones from the hare itself which "come away" easily.
— empty the rest of the stew pot into a strainer grinding up all the solids left intact (except of course the bones and the bouquet garni which should be removed).
— mix the chopped ingredients (see above) with the purée obtained after straining. If necessary, add the remainder of the second bottle of wine (since you used a bottle and a half for the first stage of cooking), so as to get a slightly runny mixture.
— Put the pieces of hare back in the cooking pot along with the mixture described above and all the bones which were removed. Cook over a low and constant heat for a second stage of cooking of 1 hour and 30 minutes.

• It is essential for the success of the recipe that by the end of the cooking time the pieces of meat are in a sauce whose consistency can be likened to that of a potato purée: neither too runny nor too thick (for the flesh of the hare is by nature very dry).

• All that remains is the final operation which must be undertaken in the minutes leading up to the dish being served at the table (the dish can, as described earlier, be prepared the night before, and then be reheated carefully prior to this final operation).

• Whisk the hare's blood vigorously so that there are no clots and mix it together with the sauce in the cooking pot. Add 250 to 300 g of uncooked foie gras, cut into medium sized cubes, arranging these across the top of the pot without mixing them in, The guests will serve themselves directly from the cooking pot which will be placed on the table. As an accompaniment, serve high quality steamed potatoes.

• In our opinion, the presence of all these different ingredients renders the use of salt and pepper totally unnecessary.

STUFFED CABBAGE

This is a typically rustic dish which is usually prepared when the weather is rather cold. Unlike the other "mythical" dishes there are not many variations to the recipe (apart, obviously, from the preparation of the stuffing). Here we give only two recipes, apart from the traditional method of preparation, both of which are quite original, are little known, and can be carried out by an amateur.

• Use a cabbage weighing about 1 kg, with a good heart.

• You can either:
— remove the stalk and the damaged outer leaves by taking off the leaves one by one, washing them carefully and blanching them in boiling water for 15 minutes. Drain them in a colander.

— or, you can scoop out the heart of the cabbage from the exterior, with a very sharp knife, by cutting away the major part of the stump whilst still taking care that the leaves remain attached. Also remove some of the larger leaf spines. In order to wash the cabbage (which is still in one piece) leave it to soak for 15 minutes in some water with vinegar in it (**why** with vinegar? to get rid of any caterpillars or worms which may be hidden between the leaves). Blanch as above. Obviously, this second method of preparation renders subsequent operations more difficult than the first method (where the leaves are entirely separate).

• You can, of course, make a stuffing by putting all of the ingredients into the mixer but it is much simpler to buy about 600 g of sausage meat, to which can be added, according to individual taste, some parsley, some garlic, some chopped onion and some pepper (quantities necessarily vary according to taste). Mix the whole lot together well.

• There are two different techniques for stuffing the cabbage depending on how the cabbage has been prepared.

• If you have detached all the leaves: line a salad bowl with a napkin and arrange the largest cabbage leaves on it, with the ribs underneath, so that it forms the first layer. Spread a layer of stuffing on top of this and then arrange another layer of smaller cabbage leaves and so on, ending with a layer of leaves. Bring the corners of the napkin together, and twist them together tightly so as to reconstitute the original shape of the cabbage. Unwrap and tip out onto a plate.

• If you have followed the second method of preparation then you will need to pull the leaves back, without breaking them, and place the stuffing between the rows of leaves. Then firmly close the leaves back up.

• For both methods: take a gratin dish and pour two tablespoons of oil into it. Next, place the cabbage in the dish, sprinkling it with a little bouillon and with 2 more tablespoons of oil. Encircle the cabbage with 4 slices of smoked bacon cut very thinly. The bouillon should not exceed three quarters of the height of the cabbage. Cook on a medium light (gas mark 6) for at least 1 hour. Keep an eye on the progress of the cooking, basting the cabbage several times with the cooking juices.

• The quality of the stuffing and its seasoning is obviously of paramount importance.

• As an extra (and as a matter of curiosity!), we shall go on to describe two other stuffings which do not use sausage meat.

• Firstly, a stuffing made with snails (tinned, why not? as long as the contents are rinsed with warm water prior to use). Take 8 dozen medium sized snails, chop them and "brown" them in a frying pan with some shallots (3) cut up with scissors, garlic (3 cloves) also cut up with scissors. Add some finely chopped button mushrooms (200 g). Cook over a low light until the juice has disappeared. Incorporate 1 whole egg and 2 egg yolks and mix together well. Stuff the cabbage as above and proceed in the same way for subsequent operations.

• Another possibility for the stuffing is: 300 g of fresh salmon cut into fairly thin strips which should be placed straight into the cabbage, as above. With this recipe, however, you must tie a piece of string round the cabbage as it has to cook in a court bouillon and it must not sink to the bottom of the pan (tie the end of the string to a piece of wood fixed across the top of the pan). For the court bouillon you will need: 1 litre of white wine, 50 cl of water, 1 carrot, thyme and bay. Bring the court bouillon to the boil and leave to simmer for 20 minutes. You can then plunge in the cabbage and leave it in the simmering court bouillon for 15 to 20 minutes. Leave the cabbage in the saucepan until you are ready to serve.

SOME EQUIVALENT WEIGHTS AND MEASURES
(APPROXIMATELY)

1 level teaspoon of fine salt	5 g
1 level teaspoon of water	5 g
1 level tablespoon of flour	12 g
1 level tablespoon of caster sugar	15 g
1 level tablespoon of rice	20 g
1 level tablespoon of oil	15 g

PRACTICAL COOKING INSTRUCTIONS

Many modern cooking appliances no longer indicate the degree of temperature reached if you slightly alter the position of the control knob and so we thought that it would be useful to provide the following conversion table:

Gas mark 1-2	105 to 150°	very low
Gas mark 3-4	150 to 190°	low
Gas mark 5-6	190 to 225°	medium
Gas mark 7-8	225 to 270°	hot
Gas mark 9-10	270 to 310°	very hot

On average, as far as the more usual cuts of meat are concerned, you should count on the following quantities per person:

Roast without bones	120 to 160 g
Roast with bones	180 to 200 g
Cutlet with bone	180 to 220 g
Cutlet without bone	160 to 200 g
Thin slices	120 to 140 g
Ragout	160 to 200 g
Knuckle/shin	180 to 240 g
Minced meat	100 to 120 g
Kidneys	130 to 150 g

SOME BASIC DEFINITIONS

BAIN-MARIE: This is a large receptacle containing boiling water, in which another smaller receptacle containing ingredients, is placed, in order that they may cook slowly without direct contact with the heat source, or for reheating.

TO BLANCH: To immerse a foodstuff for a limited amount of time in boiling water, either for a very rapid preliminary cooking (e.g. cabbage), or in order to remove salt (e.g. sausages or smoked bacon).

TO BRAISE: To cook meat, over a low light, in a closed receptacle containing a little liquid, e.g. white wine, with which the juice released by the meat itself gradually blends. If possible, you should use a casserole pot with a lid with slits in it, through which water can be added, thereby preventing foodstuffs from "sticking".

To cut with scissors : Term used as an alternative to chopping, meaning to cut into small pieces with scissors. This prevents the loss of substances which are produced when foodstuffs are chopped e.g. seasoning herbs.

«Déglacer» : To rinse the bottom of a pan, in which meat has been cooked, with a liquid (water, cream, bouillon). In this way the juices are recovered for use in sauces.

To thinly slice : To cut into thin strips.

To sweat: To cook "watery" vegetables (so called because they themselves contain water) in a very small amount of water, e.g. mushrooms, leeks, chicory etc. These vegetables produce their own juice which adds to the cooking juices.

En julienne (to cut en julienne): To cut certain vegetables into very thin strips (carrots, turnips, celery, the white part of the leek).

To coat: To cover a dish (chicken, fish, meat) with a sauce. Attention: to coat does not mean to cover excessively.

To poach: To simmer gently, without boiling, for several minutes, without a lid.

To season: To add herbs or spices, or sometimes just salt or pepper, in order to give flavour.

To brown: To quickly place some meat or vegetables in very hot fat, without letting them stick, so as to encourage the coagulation or caramelization of the surface of the produce. Synonym: to "seal".

To seal: The same as "to brown" but at a higher temperature and for a shorter period of time (sudden coagulation).

To sauté: This means to brown a foodstuff without it "sticking". The cooking receptacle must, therefore, be shaken so as to move the foodstuff.

Some particulary useful
Kitchen utensils

Conical strainer: A strainer with a very fine mesh, in the shape of a cone. It must be strong so that you can also use it to push through, and thus grind, the remaining solids left in a juice.

Vegetable knife: Knife used to peel vegetables thinly.

Casserole pot: This is a round or oval utensil which comes in lots of materials (earthenware, porcelain, ovenproof, copper, aluminium, even toughened glass). If possible you should use a casserole with a lid which has slits in it, through which water can be added, thereby stopping the meat or vegetables inside it from drying up and sticking to the bottom.

LIST OF RECIPES

Photos cover, page 8 : Didier BENAOUDA

Design
Brigitte RACINE

Cet ouvrage a été achevé d'imprimer
par l'Imprimerie Pollina à Luçon (85) - n° 67505 - B
ISBN : 2.7373.1753.3
Dépôt légal : mai 1995
N° d'éditeur : 3110.01.03.05.95